T. L. OS

THE GOOD LIFE

BOOKS BY THE OSBORNS

BELIEVERS IN ACTION—*Apostolic–Rejuvenating*

BIBLICAL HEALING—*Seven Miracle Keys*
4 Visions–50+ yrs. of Proof–324 Merged Bible Vs.

FIVE CHOICES FOR WOMEN WHO WIN
21st Century Options

GOD'S BIG PICTURE—*An Impelling Gospel Classic*

GOD'S LOVE PLAN—*The Awesome Discovery*

HEALING THE SICK—*A Living Classic*

JESUS AND WOMEN—*Big Questions Answered*

LIFE–TRIUMPH OVER TRAGEDY
A True Story of Life After Death

MIRACLES–*Proof of God's Love*

NEW LIFE FOR WOMEN—*Reality Re-focused*

NEW MIRACLE LIFE NOW
Global Communiqué of The Christian Faith

SOULWINNING-OUTSIDE THE SANCTUARY
A Classic on Biblical Christianity & Human Dignity

THE BEST OF LIFE—*Seven Energizing Dynamics*

THE GOOD LIFE—*A Mini-Bible School–1,467 Ref.*

THE GOSPEL ACCORDING TO T.L. & DAISY
Their Life & World Ministry–510 pg. Pictorial

THE MESSAGE THAT WORKS
T.L.'s Revealing Manifesto on Biblical Faith

THE POWER OF POSITIVE DESIRE
An Invigorating Faith Perspective

THE WOMAN BELIEVER
Awareness of God's Design

WOMAN WITHOUT LIMITS
Unmuzzled—Unfettered—Unimpeded

WOMEN & SELF-ESTEEM
Divine Royalty Unrestrained

YOU ARE GOD'S BEST
Transforming Life Discoveries

USA HQ:

OSBORN INTERNATIONAL

P.O. Box 10, Tulsa, OK 74102 USA

T.L. OSBORN, FOUNDER & PRES.
LADONNA OSBORN, VICE-PRES. & CEO

Tel: 918/743-6231
Fax: 918/749-0339 E-Mail: OSFO@aol.com
www.OSBORN.ORG

Canada: Box 281, Adelaide St. Post Sta., Toronto M5C 2J4
England: Box 148, Birmingham B3 2LG
(A Registered Charity)

DEDICATED

I AFFECTIONATELY dedicate this book to those who would like to know that God is GOOD and who are willing for Him to bless and prosper them with His abundance, spiritually, physically and materially.

For over five decades, Daisy, my wife, and I have ministered to audiences of from 20,000 to 300,000 and more daily in over 73 nations.

This book contains much of what we have shared with those millions of people, face to face, around the world. Now we dedicate these truths to YOU. □

Crusade photographs by
Daisy Washburn Osborn

T.L. Osborn

BIBLE QUOTATIONS IN THIS BOOK MAY BE PERSONALIZED, PARAPHRASED, ABRIDGED OR CONFORMED TO THE *PERSON* AND *TENSE* OF THEIR CONTEXTUAL APPLICATION IN ORDER TO FOSTER CLARITY AND INDIVIDUAL ACCEPTANCE. VARIOUS LANGUAGE TRANSLATIONS AND VERSIONS HAVE BEEN CONSIDERED. BIBLICAL REFERENCES ENABLE THE READER TO COMPARE THE PASSAGES WITH HIS OR HER OWN BIBLE.

THE AUTHOR

2004-11

Enlarged Edition
ISBN 0-87943-148-2

Printed in the United States of America

CONTENTS

THE OSBORN WORLD MINISTRY

THE MINISTRY OF T.L. and Daisy Osborn has made an unprecedented impact on the world. Married at ages 17 and 18, they were missionaries in India at 20 and 21. They are valued among the great soulwinners of this century.

In 1949 they instituted *OSFO International, a world evangelism and missionary church organization.*

Their life commitment: *To express and propagate the Gospel of Christ to all people throughout the world.* Their motto: One Way - *Jesus*; One Job - *Evangelism.* Their guiding principle: *The top priority of the church is the evangelization of the world.*

For over a half century together, they proclaimed the Gospel to millions, face to face, in 74 nations. (Daisy died in May, 1995.) Their crusade audiences have numbered from 25,000 to over 300,000 per meeting.

Their literature has been published in 132 languages and dialects.

They have produced docu-miracle crusade films, audio and video cassettes, crusade tapes and Bible courses for study and public evangelism in nearly 80 languages.

They have sponsored over thirty thousand qualified national preachers, both women and men, as full-time missionaries to their own and neighboring tribes and villages where the Gospel of Christ had not been established.

They have provided airlifts and huge shipments of soulwinning tools for Gospel missions and Christian workers worldwide, including scores of 4-wheel mobile vehicles equipped with films, projectors, giant screens, generators, public-address systems, audio cassettes and cassette players, and hundreds of tons of literature for evangelism abroad.

They have been prolific writers. Their books have helped to stimulate a worldwide rediscovery of apostolic miracle-evangelism.

T.L.'s living classic, *Healing the Sick,* already in its enlarged 43th edition, has been a faith-building best-seller since 1951. Over a million copies are in print.

Their 510-page classic documentary, *The Gospel According to T.L. & Daisy,* with 489 photos, tells their story.

Dr. Daisy's five major books are unmatched among Christian publications for the female members of the Body of Christ, helping women and men alike, to rediscover their *Identity, Dignity, Destiny and Equality* in God's plan for their lives.

The Osborns have probably reached and led more unreached souls to Christ in non-Christian lands, and may have witnessed more great healing miracles, than any other couple in history. Their team efforts in world evangelism have been truly pacesetting as they have proclaimed to the world the good news that *Jesus Christ is the same yesterday, to day and for ever.* [He.13:8]

Preface

MANY YEARS AGO I learned that I am what I take into myself.

My input determines my output.

The kind of seed that I plant determines the kind of harvest that I reap.

To live the GOOD LIFE, I must drink at the good fountain. This book will show you where it is and how to drink from it.

The psalmist David said: *How excellent is your lovingkindness, O God! (to those who) put their trust under your wings. They shall be abundantly satisfied, (they shall) drink at the river of your pleasure. For with you is the FOUNTAIN OF LIFE.*[Ps.36:7-9]

Solomon said: *Listen to me, and you will have a long, good life. Carry out my instructions, for they will lead you to real living.*[Pr.4:10,13 LB]

Humankind is designed to think, plan, talk and act with God — fulfilling His purpose on earth.

No state of being is as rewarding as living in harmony with God. Get His ideas. Work with His projects. See life as He sees it. Discover who you are and your own real value. See yourself as God sees you. Get interested in His plans. Get God's opinion of yourself — and of others.

When you learn what God has made you for, how He treasures your company, and the happy, healthy and prosperous lifestyle that He wills for you, you will discover the true fountain of good living.

I began discovering the truly good life when I was only twelve years old. My objectives and my motives were determined at once. I wanted what God wanted. I wanted it for the reason God wanted it. Those principles anchored me through adolescence. They guided me in marriage. They were the foundation stones of our home and the guidelines for raising our children.

These good seeds of the good life have produced for us a constant and rich harvest of happiness, health, rewarding service to others, fantastic achievement, a life of exciting love in marriage, family contentment, harmony and abundance.

I was born on a farm in Oklahoma, one of thirteen children. My wife, Daisy, was born on a farm in California, one of eleven children. At the age of twelve, we both learned about the abundant life of Jesus Christ and received Him: she in California, I in Oklahoma, over one thousand miles apart.

Immediately, I set out to share this new lifestyle with others. I printed the good life concepts on a toy press and delivered them to our neighbors.

At the age of thirteen, I was teaching Bible lessons on the good life to a class of fifteen to twenty-year olds.

At fifteen, I began speaking to crowds, traveling with a mature evangelist as his assistant.

At seventeen, I met Daisy Washburn in a church in California.

At 17 and 18 we were married.

At 20 and 21 we were missionaries in India.

At 23 and 24 we were addressing audiences of fifteen to fifty thousand people.

For nearly four decades, we have taught the principles of the good life in over 73 nations, to multitudes numbering from 20,000 to 300,000 in a single service.

Multiplied thousands have turned to Christ as a result.

Following most of our crusades, we have organized seminars for believers, as part of our follow-up program, and taught on living the good life to those who received Jesus Christ.

This book shares with you some of what we have shared with so many others around the world.

Sickness and suffering, fear and condemnation, guilt and shame, defeat and poverty are not

God's will for you.

Following the principles of His lifestyle will set you on the good road to the good life.

You will learn how to be courageous and decisive.

You will discover health and vigor.

You will prosper and be materially blessed.

You will have new friends.

People will like you.

You will overcome bad habits.

Your loved ones will benefit from your new lifestyle. You will receive solutions to your problems — and to theirs.

You will prosper financially. Your bills will be paid and you will begin to enjoy the good things you have long desired.

Old weaknesses and chronic ailments will disappear.

Sicknesses will be cured.

A new self-assurance and self-esteem will possess you.

You will succeed instead of fail.

You will get relief from pressure and tension.

Your plans will be clear.

Your sins will be forgiven. Guilt and condemnation will be gone.

Living will become a pleasure.

You will be happy and know achievement.

You will help and enrich others.

People will esteem you and believe in you.

It is all part of the good life.

As Solomon said, *You will have a long, good life, my instructions will lead you to real living* [Pr.4:10,13LB] Jesus said, *I am come that you might have LIFE ... ABUNDANTLY.* [Jn.10:10] Or as the French Bible says, *that you might have LIFE and LIVE IN ABUNDANCE.*

God wants you to have this goodness from Him.

He has many miracles in store for you. Now you can give Him a chance to prove His goodness in your life.

Good things will start unfolding in your life from this very day.

The good life is clearly set before you. Accept it and start expecting miracles.

This book, in your hands, is a sure sign that God is reaching out to you — right now.

PART

I

FOUNDATION FOR BELIEVING

HERE ARE FACTS which lift you from boring mediocrity to the success and exhilarating self-esteem which develops when you discover who you are.

From the breathtaking grandeur of mountain peaks to the fabulous wealth of rich valleys, the Lord God has indeed placed man and woman amidst a world of good things.

Unless life has total meaning with God, it becomes a total mess without God.

I saw the Lord myself -- ALIVE. He came into my room at six o'clock one morning and I looked on Him as clearly as I can see anyone. ➡

Chapter 1

Paradise of Abundance

THE VAST WEALTH of this planet is the creation of God who is good [Ps.145:8-9; Ps.100:5; Ps.119:68] and who has created an abundance of good things for you.

Every diamond and precious stone, every mineral and every natural treasure is placed here, on deposit, for the good life which God wills for you.[De.33:13-16; Ez.28:13]

From the flamboyant tulip beds which dazzle the landscapes of Holland to the lush orchid masses of tropical jungles, God has decked our environment with splendor and beauty.

From the breathtaking grandeur of mountain peaks to the fabulous wealth of rich valleys, the Lord God has indeed placed man and woman amidst a world of abundance.

Adam and Eve were created and placed in the Garden of Eden — a paradise of abundance. Made in God's own image, they were destined to live and dream and work with God, carrying out His divine plan on earth.[Ge.1:26-31]

Then temptation came.[Ge.3:1-6] Man and woman sinned and were consequently driven out of God's presence [Ge.3:22-24] to become the slaves of Satan. They forfeited their right to the good life.

God, in His love, never abandoned His dream of having man and woman, whom He had created in His own image, near Him. But being righteous, God could not fellowship with sin.[Is.59:1-2]

His law was made and it could not be compromised. *The soul that sins, it shall die.*[Ez.18:4,20] All had sinned so all must die.[Ro.5:12]

But to satisfy the claims of justice, one who was perfectly innocent could take the place of the guilty and die as a substitute. Once the punishment was suffered by a perfect and innocent substitute, the crime of the guilty would be paid for, and the guilty one could be justified as though no sin had been committed.[Ro.5:1]

Jesus Christ, God's Son, was perfect. He had never sinned. He came to this world and took upon Himself the sins of the whole world and suffered our full penalty.[Jn.1:29]

God loved the world so much that he gave his only begotten Son, that whoever believes in him should not perish but have everlasting life.[Jn.3:16]

All that will ever be required of you to receive total justification before God, is that you simply believe with all your heart that Jesus Christ died in your stead. Respond to such love by willingly confessing to others what you believe.[Ro.10:9-10]

Once you comprehend the good news of what Jesus did for you and once you believe it with your heart and confess it to others, an incredible miracle takes place: *God took the sinless Christ and poured into him your sins. Then, in exchange, he pours God's goodness into you.*[2Co.5:21 LB]

Jesus Christ became your way back to God.

Through His sacrifice, He removed forever the condemnation of your sins and dissolved the barrier between you and God, so that you are now welcome to return to His presence where you can once again share the good life.[He.10:18-22]

Human persons are created in God's image. They are God's kind of being. They can never find full satisfaction without God. Loneliness and grief, sickness and suffering, poverty and failure, hatred and murder are all evidence that humanity has lost its way.

People instinctively seek God. They long for a meaningful life. Their lives have divine purpose and until they discover that purpose, they live in a void. Uncertainty makes them pessimistic.

When Rear Admiral Richard Byrd lost his bearings in the antarctic night, the awful realization came over him that he had missed the way. He later said, "I knew I was lost, and I felt sick inside."

Even a bold exterior cannot hide the inner emptiness and loss of direction. Like a blind person tapping a cane on the sidewalk, the modern person taps from event to event, from day to day, in search of the right way.

Jesus said, *I AM THE WAY.*[Jn.14:6]

He is not **a** way. He is **the** way, because He is the one who took our place and bore the punishment of our sins, so that nothing could stand between us and God.[1Pe.2:24] Now we can come home — to the garden of His abundance for which we were created, and live the good life God lovingly wills for us.[Jn.10:10]

No good thing will he withhold from them that walk uprightly before him.[Ps.84:11]

For as you know him better, he will give you, through his great power, everything you need for living a truly good life: he even shares his own goodness with us.[2Pe.1:3 LB]

There will be no more fear, uncertainty, guilt, condemnation or inferiority before God. You will know Him and fellowship with Him as a personal friend — even closer, as a member of His own household.[Ep.2:18-19]

Sickness, suffering and disease will no longer intrude because Jesus Christ will make His home at your house.[Jn.14:23] He becomes your health, as

His life is manifested in your physical body.[2Co.4:10] You become God's property.[1Co.6:20] Your body is not created for infirmities and illnesses. It is the temple of the Holy Ghost.[1Co.6:19]

Poverty and material deprivation, lack and insufficiency will no longer be your lot in life. God created the wealth of this planet and He placed it here for the prosperity of His children. The abundance which He created all around you is proof that He wills the good life for you. He promises *to supply all your need according to his riches, by Christ Jesus.*[Ph.4:19]

His word says, *I wish above all things that you may prosper and be in health, even as your soul prospers.*[3Jn.2]

My purpose is to give life in all of its fullness.[Jn.10:10 FB]

I will cure them, and will reveal to them the abundance of peace and truth. I will cleanse them from their iniquity and I will pardon all their iniquities where they have transgressed against me. They shall fear and tremble for all the goodness and for all the prosperity that I do for my people.[Je.33:6-9 LB]

Instead of shame and dishonor, you shall have a double portion of prosperity and everlasting joy, and all shall realize that you are a people God has blessed.[Is.61:7,9 LB]

Peter said, *If you want a happy, good life, quietly*

trust yourself to Christ your Lord and if anybody asks why you believe as you do, be ready to tell them, and do it in a gentle and respectful way.[1Pe.3:10,15 LB]

This book is inspired of God to help you do that.

The good life is God's gold mine for you, here and now.

God **is** what He says He is.

You **are** what He says you are.

God **will** do what He says He will do.

You **can** do what He says you can do.

God **has** what He says He has.

You **have** what He says you have.

Chapter 2

Why I Believe the Bible is True

TO REALLY LIVE the good life, your faith must rest upon your absolute belief in the Bible as the inspired word of God. I want to share with you five basic reasons why I believe the Bible is true.

I have written them for ordinary people who want to believe the Bible. I could fill a volume with theological data, yet never convince anyone who is not willing to believe.

When Christ raised Lazarus from the dead, some took counsel to kill Him. Even the raising of one from the dead could not outweigh their own prejudices, and human nature has not changed. That is why I say these are simple, practical reasons for faith in the Bible. They are expressed to help you believe and live the happy life God planned for you.

I BELIEVE the Bible is true because of its content and harmony.

Forty different herdsmen, shepherds, fishermen, politicians, princes, poets, philosophers, statesmen, prophets, priests, publicans and physicians who lived during nearly two millenniums, penned some 66 different books on the subjects of history, poetry, prophesy, letters, proverbs, parables, allegories and orations.

These diverse writers, spanning various cultures and traditions, wrote from different countries separated by hundreds of miles, extending through two continents. There is no discord and not a flaw of incoherency. Yet these writings contain one system of doctrine, one plan of salvation, one order of ethics, one rule of faith, and one story of love and redemption.

Separated by hundreds of miles and spread through centuries of time, 40 different authors, both women and men, wrote from Syria, Arabia, Italy, Greece, the desert of Sinai, the wilderness of Judea, the cave of the prison of Rome, the Isle of Patmos, the palaces of Mt. Zion and Shushan, the rivers of Babylon and the banks of the Chedar. How could they have possibly conceived such unity and cohesion of thought?

Could that many writers from that many cultures conceive a common deception? It is hardly thinkable, and that logic causes me to trust their writings and to believe that what they said and recorded was inspired of God for the good of humankind.

It has been tested for twenty centuries. History has no record of any person or society who ever attempted to improve it. Not a shred of archaeological evidence has yet contradicted it, but has only put to shame those who have ridiculed it. The more I read it, the more I believe it.

Scientists who doubt it cannot prove its error. To the contrary, every new scientific discovery was already evidenced by the Bible.

Scientists have made innumerable errors. Until a few hundred years ago they believed that the earth was flat. As late as 1890, a great technician said, "Common sense tells you that if a horseless vehicle is built that travels 50 miles an hour, the driver would not be able to get his breath." Not long ago high blood pressure was treated by draining blood from the patient.

But the word of the Lord endures forever. And this is the word which by the gospel is preached to you. [1Pe.1:25]

I BELIEVE the Bible is true because of the witness of martyrs.

People and governments have repeatedly sought to obliterate faith in God. Christians have been persecuted mercilessly, tortured ruthlessly; Bibles have been burned, its messengers have been stoned, fed to wild animals, boiled in oil; they have killed its prophets, and murdered its followers. [He.11:32-38; Re.6:9]

But *this multitude of witnesses,*[He.12:1-3] both women and men, who have died for their testimony of Jesus Christ, all held to His principle of love. They never retaliated, never became vengeful, never rendered evil for good, never wished calamity for their persecutors. They lived and died in love. *They did not love their lives but laid them down for him.*[Re.12:11 LB]

They believed the words of Jesus: *That you love one another; as I have loved you.*[Jn.13:34] *A servant is not greater than their lord.*[Jn.13:16] *We know what real love is from Christ's example in dying for us. And so we also ought to lay down our lives for other believers.*[1Jn.3:16 LB] *The greatest love is shown when a person lays down their life for a friend.*[Jn.15:13 LB]

When such a multitude of people have laid down their lives in love for their testimony of the gospel, I am impressed. It is more than a political or a religious cause. It has to be something of profound reality.

I BELIEVE the Bible is true because of the people who taught me to believe it.

Christians were among the finest people of our community.

They were not the rapists, the sexually perverted, the rioters, the thieves; they were not the ones who failed to pay their debts or who were dishonest in business; they never revolted or destroyed property.

They were the peaceful, good, loving people – the backbone of our society. I could trust them. They would rather die than deceive me. They were the builders, not the destroyers. They were the hard workers, not the lazy riffraff. Their homes and lives were clean and pure and loving.

They were not beating nor abusing their companions or children. Their families prayed and worked together. Love ruled their households.

All of that impressed me.

They believed the Bible. They lived by its sacred principles. I could trust them. The fruit of their lives was what I wanted.

I BELIEVE the Bible is true because of the life of Christ.

Jesus Christ was a good man. He was kind and loving; a man of peace and of good works. He cared for every individual, regardless of age, social or economic status, color, race or sex.

He advocated principles that are the cornerstones of the best and the most free societies in history. He never hated or envied. He never sought for revenge or passed judgment. He loved and healed and helped and encouraged.

He identified with those who had no friends. He loved the most unlovely and blessed the most unworthy.

His rules of life were the most challenging of any leader who ever lived.

Treat others as you want them to treat you.[Lu.6:31LB]

He said: *Love your enemies, bless them that curse you, do good to them that hate you, and pray for them which despitefully use you, and persecute you; that you may be the children of your Father which is in heaven.*[Mt.5:44-45]

Jesus believed the scriptures. He quoted them as being the absolute word of God. He lived by them, taught them, proved them, made them work. He was good and honest, without guile or deceit. I can trust Him more than any other teacher.

When He healed lepers, sick people and raised the dead, unbelievers tried to kill Him. When cripples walked, he was accused of curing by the devil's power. When He helped people in need, they plotted His destruction. And even today in some areas, those who do not believe the Bible are often vehement, violent, ruthless against the Christian faith. They seem to hate simple faith and wish its destruction, as though the peace and love and healing influence of Jesus Christ might obstruct their own influence on society.

Finally, opposers and haters of Jesus told so many lies about Christ and laid so many plots to destroy Him, that they succeeded in getting license to crucify Him.

Throughout the cruel process of His trial and the false accusations against Him, He never retaliated or became harsh or unkind. In His dying moments He prayed for their forgiveness.[Lu.23:34]

Pilate said, *I find no fault in this man.*[Lu.23:4] Indeed He had no faults. He was perfect. I can trust Him and can trust what He said.

Jesus said that people *err, not knowing the scriptures.*[Mt.22:29] *The scriptures must be fulfilled.*[Mk.14:49] He *expounded to them all the scriptures.*[Lu.24:27] *He opened to* (people) *the scriptures that they might understand them.*[Lu.24:32,45] He said to *search the scriptures,*[Jn.5:39] and asked the religious teachers if *they had not read the scriptures.*[Mk.12:10] When He did miracles and taught, He said it was *that the scripture might be fulfilled.*[Jn.13:18; Jn.17:12; Jn.19:24,28,36]

Ninety times in the New Testament, there are admonitions for us to believe what is written because it is God's word and it will come to pass.

Jesus proved the scriptures. His birth, life, death and resurrection as well as His teachings and miracles were foretold in detail, hundreds of years earlier, in the scriptures.

All that Christ did proved that the scriptures were God's word — God's promises, and that if anyone would trust them and rely upon them,

God would fulfill them. That is a very good reason for believing the Bible, especially when weighed against the confusion, changing conclusions and endless quandary of those who reject the truth of the Bible.

Good sense influences me to trust Jesus, and to trust the good, stalwart Christians of every generation since Christ. Prudence causes me to believe the Bible.

I BELIEVE the Bible is true because of what happened after the crucifixion.

After His death and burial, the English Living Bible says: *He appeared from time to time, actually alive, and proved to them in many ways that it was really he himself they were seeing.*[Ac.1:3]

They saw Him and touched Him and talked with Him. They watched Him eat bread and fish. They examined the scars in His hands and feet and side. They did all of this after He arose from the dead.[Jn.20:14,20; Jn.20:26-27; Jn.21:4-14; Lu.24:13-15; Lu.24:30-31; Lu.24:36-46]

Stephen saw Him.[Ac.7:54-60]

Saul of Tarsus, the ruthless persecutor of the early believers, saw the Lord,[Ac.9:2-8; Ac.26:13-15] and became a humble follower of Christ.

Cephas saw Him. Five hundred people saw Him at one time. James saw Him, and all of the apostles saw Him.[1Co.15:5-7]

Their lives were reputed for impeccable honesty and uprightness of character.

Throughout nearly twenty centuries a countless host of witnesses have recorded their testimony that the Lord appeared to them. They saw Him alive.

Great volumes of books would be required to contain the appearances of Christ to individuals even in this century.

I wish to add to the immense volume of witnesses, my own testimony. I saw the Lord myself – alive. He came into my room at six o'clock one morning and I looked on Him as clearly as I can see anyone.

Since that experience, my wife and I have traveled and proclaimed the gospel to multitudes of 20,000 to 300,000 people and more in over 73 nations, for over five decades.

In almost every crusade we have ever conducted someone, and frequently many, have seen the Lord in our midst – always blessing, saving, healing and helping people.

A Moslem in Indonesia saw Him appear in our Djakarta crusade and saw His blood flowing from His body as He hung on the cross. That Moslem became a follower of Jesus.

A Hindu in India saw Him in our Lucknow crusade, and his blind eyes received sight.

A blind man in our Camaguey, Cuba crusade saw Him in a bright light and recovered his sight.

In Chile, a famous criminal by profession, saw Him in our Santiago crusade and was transformed into a faithful Christian. An alcoholic father who beat his children in Guatemala saw Him in our crusade there and was converted. And the miserable, outcast woman, dying of cancer, saw Him in that same crusade and was instantly cured.

In Thailand, over one hundred Buddhists saw the Lord Jesus at the same time, standing above the crusade audience. Could one hundred Buddhists lie about seeing Christ? Most of them were converted that night.

An agnostic businessman in Holland saw Jesus in our crusade in The Hague and became a vibrant Christian. The Gypsy night club singer in France saw Him in our crusade in Lille and became a gospel preacher.

Only recently, I listened to one of America's scientists testify on a coast-to-coast telecast about the experience he had when he saw the Lord standing at the right hand of the throne of God (as Stephen testified) [*Ac.7:56*] and he accepted Christ and was born again. He appealed to all scientists to have faith in God.

One of America's foremost communist insurrectionists was later converted to Jesus Christ. He had actually been living in self-imposed exile for seven years. It was while he was in the south of France that he began to be concerned about his life and that of his little son. As he looked up into the heavens, he saw the Lord Jesus Christ who appeared before him. He fell to his knees and was born again.

I think these are very valid reasons to believe the Bible. For nearly four decades we have witnessed the same miracles that Jesus experienced during His earthly ministry. These things prove that *He is the same yesterday, and to day and for ever.*[He.13:8]

In Jamaica we saw 125 deaf mutes restored. In just one crusade in Japan, 45 deaf mutes were made whole. Sixty-two blind people received sight in Kenya, over 40 in Nigeria, 30 in Indonesia. Eleven lepers were cured in Puerto Rico, 14 in Africa, 8 in South America.

Piles of crutches and braces were left behind in New York, in Chile, in Colombia. Scores of tumors and cancers were healed in Trinidad and Costa Rica, in Holland and France. Around the world for nearly four decades, we have seen proof that the Bible is true.

That is why I believe the Bible, because of all that has happened since the resurrection of Christ.

The Bible is God's word. It is true.

When the miracles of Christ were recorded, John said: *Many other signs truly did Jesus in the presence of his disciples, which are not written in this book. But these are written, that you might believe that Jesus is the Christ, the Son of God, and that believing you might have life through his name.*[Jn.20:30-31]

When the multitude of sick and demon possessed people were healed by Christ, the Bible says that it was done, *that it might be fulfilled which was spoken by Isaiah the prophet, saying, Himself took our infirmities, and bore our sicknesses.*[Mt.8:17]

Miracles were proof that the scriptures were true then. They still are — and the knowledge of miracles is abundant, even in this century, thanks to the press, the radio and the television.

A noted scientist said recently: "Everything in the absolutes of science is falling apart. We simply must return to God and the Bible. There is no other answer to the fundamental issues of life."

Chapter 3

Facts of the Good Life

WHEN YOU DISCOVER your roots in God and identify with His purpose for you on this earth, you have begun to really live the good life.

It is a lifestyle based on positive faith, positive thinking, positive talking, positive acting.

What is the source of this positive faith?

Faith comes by hearing the word of God. Ro.10:17

Here are fifty-two facts which lift you from boring mediocrity to a fruitful partnership with God. They are the miracle stepping stones that lead you from the condemning guilt-complex of living out of harmony and out of contact with God to the success and exhilarating self-esteem which develops when you discover who you are and how you can come to God and share His lifestyle.

You discover a new power, a new goal and purpose. You are transformed from defeat to success, from sickness to health, from boredom to enthusiasm, from problems to solutions, from pressure to pleasure, from poverty to prosperity, from hopelessness to happiness.

You are blessed, and your family is benefited too.

The Bible says: *Old things are passed away; behold, all things are become new.* [2Co.5:17]

These fifty-two facts will guide you to the good life. Then they become the foundation stones of God's pact of plenty — His full life policy that covers you and your house.

Review them often. Rehearse them in prayer. Memorize them. Recite them in family worship. Recount them to relatives and to friends. Enumerate them. They will keep you living the good life as you keep them in your heart and on your lips.

Anyone who embarks on this good life will, sooner or later, discover a very real enemy. The Bible calls him Satan and mentions him at least 175 times by such names as *Lucifer,* [Is.14:12-14] *the devil,* [Mt.4:1; Ep.6:11] and *Satan,* [Re.12:9] *the adversary,* [1Pe.5:8] *the god of this world,* [2Co.4:4] *the enemy,* [Mt.13:39] *the tempter,* [Mt.4:3] *the wicked one,* [Mt.13:19] *the ruler of darkness,* [Ep.6:12] *the murderer,* [Jn.8:44] and by other names.

You will meet him in his most subtle form as *the accuser.* [Re.12:10]

So when you are discouraged, or tempted to doubt your experience with God, rehearse these fifty-two facts of the good life.

That is the effective way to *resist the devil,* and James said *he will flee from you.*[Ja.4:7]

The apostle John said, *They overcame* (Satan) *by the word of their testimony;* [Re.12:11] and Jesus defeated every temptation of Satan by saying, *It is written,*[Mt.4:4,7,10] then by quoting a scripture.

When the accuser tempts you, rehearse these facts and confess these scriptures and it will happen to you as it did to Jesus: *Then the devil left him, and, behold, angels came and ministered to him.*[Mt.4:11]

So, learn these facts and make these verses your confession:

1. You were unsaved before you received Christ.

For all have sinned, and come short of the glory of God.[Ro.3:23]

2. You were guilty before God, under the penalty of death.

For the wages of sin is death.[Ro.6:23]

3. But God loved you too much to see you perish.

He is not willing that any should perish, but that all should come to repentance.[2Pe.3:9]

4. God offered His best to prove His love to you.

God so loved the world that he gave his only begot-

ten Son, that whoever believes in him shall not perish, but have everlasting life.[Jn.3:16]

5. Christ was God's gift and He died for you.

But God commends his love toward us, in that while we were yet sinners, Christ died for us.[Ro.5:8]

6. You realize that your sins separated you from God.

Your iniquities have separated between you and your God, and your sins have hid his face from you.[Is.59:2]

7. Knowing your sins cost God His Son, and Jesus His life and blood, you repent of them.

You sorrowed to repentance; for godly sorrow works (toward) *repentance*[2Co.7:9-10] and you know that *except you repent, you shall perish.*[Lu.13:3]

8. You confess your sins to Him and are cleansed.

If we confess our sins, he is faithful and just to forgive us our sins, and to cleanse us from all unrighteousness.[1Jn.1:9]

9. You recognize Jesus at the door of your heart. You open it and He comes in.

Behold, I stand at the door, and knock: if you hear my voice, and open the door, I will come in and will sup with you and you with me[Re.3:20] (meaning to dine and have fellowship together).

10. You receive Jesus and become God's child.

As many as received Jesus Christ, to them he gave power to become the children of God, even to them that believe on his name.[Jn.1:12]

11. You become a new creature.

If any one be in Christ that one is a new creature: old things are passed away; behold, all things are become new.[2Co.5:17]

12. You know you are born again because you receive Christ.

Jesus said, *You must be born again*[Jn.3:7] *and when you received Christ with power to become God's child,*[Jn.1:12] you were *born, not of blood, nor of the will of the flesh, nor of the will of a human being, but of God,*[Jn.1:13] *by the word of God which lives forever.*[1Pe.1:23]

13. You believe the powerful message of the gospel that saves you.

The gospel is the power of God to salvation to every one that believes.[Ro.1:16]

14. You believe on the name of Jesus Christ because of the record of the Gospels.

These are written, that you might believe that Jesus is the Christ, the Son of God; and that believing you might have life through his name.[Jn.20:31]

15. You call on His name and are saved.

Whoever shall call upon the name of the Lord shall

be saved.[Ro.10:13]

16. You recognize that Jesus is the only way to God.

I am the way, the truth and the life: no one comes to the Father but by me[Jn.14:6] *for there is one God, and one mediator between God and people, the man Christ Jesus.*[1Ti.2:5]

17. You know there is salvation in none other.

Neither is there salvation in any other: for there is none other name under heaven given among men, whereby we must be saved.[Ac.4:12]

18. You put your faith in Jesus as Savior.

For by grace are you saved through faith; and that not of yourselves: it is the gift of God: not of works, lest any one should boast.[Ep.2:8-9]

19. You believe that the Lord comes into your life.

I will dwell in them, and walk in them; and I will be their God, and they shall be my people. I will be a Father to you, and you shall be my sons and daughters, says the Lord Almighty.[2Co.6:16,18]

20. You do not trust in any good works or self-righteousness to be saved.

Our righteousnesses are like filthy rags.[Is.64:6] Our salvation was *not of works, lest any one should boast.*[Ep.2:9]

21. You are saved only by God's mercy.

Not by works of righteousness which we have done, but according to his mercy he saved us, by the washing of regeneration, and renewing of the Holy Ghost; Which he shed on us abundantly through Jesus Christ our Savior; That being justified by his grace, we should be made heirs according to the hope of eternal life.[Ti.3:5-7]

22. You know Christ's death justifies you before God.

Being justified by faith, we have peace with God through our Lord Jesus Christ.[Ro.5:1]

23. You know His blood remits your sins forever.

This is my blood which is shed for many for the remission of sins.[Mt.26:28] *Being justified by his blood, we shall be saved from wrath through him.*[Ro.5:9]

24. You know you are cleansed from sin.

To him that loved us, and washed us from our sins in his own blood; [Re.1:5] *In whom we have redemption through his blood, even the forgiveness of sins.*[Co.1:14]

25. You know your sins are put away and forgotten.

Behold the Lamb of God, which takes away the sin of the world,[Jn.1:29] having *removed our transgressions from us as far as the east is from the west* [Ps.103:12] so that *your sins and iniquities will he remember no more.*[He.10:17]

26. You know your sins were paid for by Christ's death.

Who his own self bore our sins in his own body on the tree, that we, being dead to sins, should live to righteousness.[1Pe.2:24] *He was wounded for our transgressions. He was bruised for our iniquities: the chastisement of our peace was upon him.*[Is.53:5]

27. With your sins punished and washed away you know they can never condemn you again.

There is therefore now no condemnation to them which are in Christ Jesus,[Ro.8:1] *for God made him who knew no sin, to be sin for us; that we might be made the righteousness of God in Christ* [2Co.5:21] and *where remission is, there is no more offering for sin* [He.10:18] so that now nothing *shall separate us from the love of Christ.*[Ro.8:35]

28. You know when you accept Christ you receive His life.

Those that have the Son have life,[1Jn.5:12] *for they that hear my word, and believe on him that sent me, have everlasting life, and shall not come into condemnation, but you are passed from death to life.*[Jn.5:24] *And this is life eternal, that they might know you the only true God, and Jesus Christ whom you have sent.*[Jn.17:3]

29. You know Satan will accuse you.

He is the accuser which accused them before our God day and night[Re.12:10] just like he did to Job.[Jb.1:6-12]

30. You are not ignorant of His works.

Lest Satan should get an advantage of us: for we are not ignorant of his devices.[2Co.2:11] For we know that he *comes to steal, and to kill, and to destroy.*[Jn.10:10]

31. You know how Jesus overcame him.

But he answered and said, it is written.[Mt.4:4,7,10] *Then the devil left him, and, behold, angels came and ministered to him.*[Mt.4:11]

32. You know Jesus proved that Satan could not win.

Christ was in all points tempted like we are, yet without sin. Let us therefore come boldly to the throne of grace, that we may obtain mercy, and find grace to help in time of need.[He.4:15-16]

33. You know He faithfully helps you in temptation.

There is no temptation taken you but such as is common to humankind: but God is faithful, who will not suffer you to be tempted above that you are able; but will with the temptation also make a way to escape, that you may be able to bear it.[1Co.10:13]

34. You know that there are two weapons Satan can never resist.

And they overcame him (the devil who accused them before God day and night) *by the blood of the Lamb, and by the word of their testimony.*[Re.12:11]

35. You know Satan cannot win over your faith.

Be sober, be vigilant; because your adversary the devil, as a roaring lion, walks about, seeking whom he may devour: Whom resist steadfast in the faith.[1Pe.5:8-9] *Resist the devil, and he will flee from you. Draw near to God, and he will draw near to you;* [Ja.4:7-8] *you who are the begotten of God keep yourself, and that wicked one touches you not.*[1Jn.5:18]

36. You know your faith is the victory.

For whoever is born of God overcomes the world: and this is the victory that overcomes the world, even our faith.[1Jn.5:4]

37. You know not to love the world but to do God's will.

Love not the world, neither the things that are in the world. If any one love the world, the love of the Father is not in them. For all that is in the world, the lust of the flesh, and the lust of the eyes, and the pride of life, is not of the Father, but is of the world. And the world passes away, and the lust thereof; but those who do the will of God live for ever.[1Jn.2:15-17]

38. You know Christ came to defeat your enemy.

For this purpose the Son of God was manifested, that he might destroy the works of the devil.[1Jn.3:8]

39. You know Satan is no match for Christ in you.

Christ in you, the hope of glory.[Co.1:27] *I will dwell in you and walk in you, says the Lord Almighty.*[2Co.6:16,18] *You are of God, little children and have overcome, because greater is he that is in you than he that is in the world.*[1Jn.4:4]

40. You know your new life source is the Lord Jesus Christ.

I am crucified with Christ: nevertheless I live; yet not I, but Christ lives in me: and the life which I now live in the flesh I live by the faith of the Son of God, who loved me, and gave himself for me.[Ga.2:20]

41. You know your new life has divine purpose.

The steps of good people are ordered by the Lord and God delights in their way. Though they fall, they shall not be utterly cast down: for the Lord upholds them with his hand.[Ps.37:23-24]

42. You know God sees you and hears you.

For the eyes of the Lord are over the righteous and his ears are open to their prayers.[1Pe.3:12]

43. You know He invites you to call on Him.

Call to me, and I will answer you.[Je.33:3] *Ask, and it shall be given you; seek, and you shall find; knock, and it shall be opened to you. For every one that asks receives.*[Lu.11:9-10]

44. You know when you pray that He answers.

Whatever you desire, when you pray, believe that you receive them, and you shall have them;[Mk.11:24] *and whatever you shall ask in my name, that will I do, that the Father may be glorified in the Son.*[Jn.14:13]

45. You know that you belong to God's royal family.

You are a chosen generation, a royal priesthood, an holy nation, a peculiar people; that you should show forth the praises of him who has called you out of darkness into his marvelous light.[1Pe.2:9]

46. You know that all Christ has now belongs to you.

For all who are led by the spirit of God are children of God. And so we should not be like cringing, fearful slaves, but we should behave like God's very own children, adopted into the bosom of his family, and calling him, "Father, Father" For his Holy Spirit speaks to us deep in our hearts, and tells us that we really are God's children. And since we are his children, we will share his treasures – for all God gives to his Son Jesus is now ours too.[Ro.8:14-17 LB]

47. You know you have His life in your flesh now.

That the life of Jesus might be made manifest in our mortal flesh,[2Co.4:11] for *your body is the temple of the Holy Ghost.*[1Co.6:19; 1Co.3:16-17]

48. You know you never need to live in want again.

My God shall supply all your need according to his riches in glory by Christ Jesus,[Ph.4:19] for *no good thing will he withhold from them that walk uprightly.*[Ps.84:11]

49. You no longer fear diseases and plagues.

There shall no evil befall you, neither shall any plague come near your dwelling,[Ps.91:10] because *I am the Lord who heals you.*[Ex.15:26] *Jesus took our infirmities and bore our sicknesses*[Mt.8:17] and *with his stripes we are healed.*[Is.53:5; 1Pe.2:24]

50. You no longer are oppressed by problems.

Casting all your care upon him; for he cares for you.[1Pe.5:7]

51. You know you are a winner.

If God be for us, who can be against us?[Ro.8:31] *No, in all these things we are more than conquerors through him that loved us.*[Ro.8:37] *He which has begun a good work in you will perform it until the day of Jesus Christ.*[Ph.1:6] *Faithful is he that calls you, who also will do it.*[1Th.5:24]

52. You know Christ is with you to the end.

For he has said, I will never leave you, nor forsake you. So that we may boldly say, The Lord is my helper, and I will not fear what any person shall do to me,[He.13:5-6] *and, lo, I am with you alway, even to the end of the world.*[Mt.28:20]

PART

II

THE NEW LIFESTYLE

PEOPLE AND THE devil will try to discourage you, but you and God are able to work wonders together.

I learned that as long as I do all of the talking, God will not interrupt. I discovered that God needs no interpreter. He is a masterful communicator.

There are just two essentials in life: 1) what you believe and 2) what you do as a result of it.

The man in the Russian famine and the gold digger from Australia reveal the real secrets of how to live the happy, successful and vibrant life. ➡

Chapter 4

Three Habits of the Good Life

HOW WONDERFUL TO KNOW that you are right with God. Your record is clear. No sin that you have ever committed can ever condemn you again.[Ro.8:1] You have come to Christ and received Him.[Jn.6:37; Jn.1:12] You have confessed your sins to Him and trusted His blood to cleanse you.[1Jn.1:9] He has heard your prayer and has come to live at your house.[Jn.14:23]

Never let Satan cause you to doubt your salvation. You did your part. Christ has done His part. Now *it is finished,* as Christ said when He died on the cross.[Jn.19:30]

To help you live a happy, successful Christian life, here is a daily formula – three things to do each day of your life.

If you will do these consistently, you will grow stronger and always be courageous. You will always be a happy and successful and an enthusiastic Christian.[Co.1:10-14; 2Pe.3:18]

It is easy to form these three Christian habits. They will become as natural as combing your hair, dressing yourself or eating your meals.

They gradually become part of your daily life.[Ep.4:13-15] You must be willing for changes in your lifestyle.[Ep.4:22-32; Ep.5:1-2; Co.3:12-17] Then be resolved to practice them — like a good athlete who disciplines the body with physical exercise in order to achieve higher goals.

In order to learn how to serve God and really live the good life, here are the three habits to form:

FIRST: Talk to God every day.

SECOND: Let God talk to you every day.

THIRD: Talk to someone else about God every day.

They are simple, basic, and easy to remember.

In the following three chapters, I will show you how valuable these three good habits will be for you.

Chapter 5

When God Listens to You

TALK TO GOD EVERY DAY.

That is prayer.

When you received Christ, you became part of God's family – one of His own. Now you can call God your *Father,* and He calls you His child.[2Co.6:18; Ga.4:6-7]

He wants to spend time with you like any good parent desires time with their children.[1Co.1:91Jn.1:3]

Prayer is that intimate time with your Father who is always waiting for those precious moments of communion with you.[1Pe.3:12]

I love the Lord because he hears my prayers and answers them. Because he bends down and listens, I will pray as long as I breathe.[Ps.116:1-2 LB]

He is always thinking about you and watching everything that concerns you.[1Pe.5:7 LB]

There is nothing mystical or difficult about prayer. God is your Father. You are His child. He invites you to pray and He promises to answer. So, every time you pray, you are accepting His loving invitation to come to Him and talk things over with Him. He is your best friend.

Call to me and I will answer you.[Je.33:3]

Ask, and it shall be given you, every one that asks, receives.[Lu.11:9-10]

In everything by prayer and supplication with thanksgiving, let your requests be made known to God.[Ph.4:6]

For we have not an high priest which cannot be touched with the feeling of our infirmities; but was in all points tempted like we are, yet without sin. Let us therefore come boldly to the throne of grace, that we may obtain mercy, and find grace to help in the time of need.[He.4:15-16]

So, every day, talk to your Father.

Find a convenient time and a place that is quiet, where you will not be disturbed. Jesus arose early in the morning to pray.[Mk.1:35] Before you go to bed is also a good time to pray.[Ps.55:17]

On the farm, as a lad, I prayed in the barn, down by the spring, in the woods, in the field.

Since my wife and I were first married, we have begun our days by arising at six o'clock each morning. We give our first two hours to prayer, Bible study and physical exercise. I can tell you, it pays to pray.

There is a saying: "The family that prays together stays together." When you learn to talk things over with your Lord, to tell Him your problems, needs, desires, He always has the answer, the solution, the remedy. You will be amazed at how you will experience happiness and success because you pray each day.[Ps.91:15] There is no substitute for this regular time of communion with your Father.

You may think you cannot pray. Or you might be embarrassed, not knowing what to say. Let me assure you that you need no traditional phrases or special rituals.

Begin by greeting Him.

Tell Him why you love Him. Recount what He did for you on the cross. Thank Him for each act of substitution. Tell Him what it means to you to know that Jesus went to that cross, that He suffered in your place. Talk about His suffering, His death, His burial and resurrection. Recount it all in His presence and identify with it. Then thank Him.

You will find yourself worshiping Him as you think of His blood washing away your sins and of Him raising again for your justification.

Just talk to Him about it.

Praise His name in prayer and worship.

You may read some scripture verses and express your thanks to Him for them. Thank Him for what He has done, for what He is doing right now and for what He will do for you as long as you trust in Him.

You may want to confess to Him some error you have made, some temptation you yielded to, some remark you made that hurt someone, some act which offended, something you said that brought disgrace or shame to Christ, some thought or word or deed that was not pleasing to the Lord.

The person that covers their sins shall not prosper: but whoever confesses and forsakes them shall have mercy.[Pr.28:13]

If we say we have no sin, we deceive ourselves, and the truth is not in us. If we confess our sins, he is faithful and just to forgive us our sins, and to cleanse us from all unrighteousness.[1Jn.1:8-9]

So tell Him all about it. Do not hide anything.

Then thank Him for the blood of Jesus that cleanses you and ask for the power of the Holy Spirit in your life to help you overcome temptation. Talk to Him like any child would talk to a parent or a close friend. Have confidence that He loves you.

You can talk to Him about your family and each particular need. You can pray for others, for friends and neighbors who have spiritual or physical or material needs.

Do not just think about your own affairs, but be in-

terested in others too, and in what they are doing.[Ph.2:4 LB]

Talk to God about friends or loved ones who need to be saved. Pray for them.

If you will do that each day, it will not be long before each time you face a problem or crisis of some kind, you will feel the need for His help. You will take time to tell Him about it, and you will discover that He will answer your prayers, solve your problems, meet your need, heal your sickness, defeat your enemy, and bless you more and more.

Learn to talk to Him as your best personal friend.

You do not need to be at any certain place or in any particular position to pray. If you cannot find a place where you can be alone, you do not even have to pray audibly. You can pray as you ride or drive or work. The important thing is to pray.

Do not learn prayer phrases or confine yourself to written prayers. It is better to pray from your heart. The gospel of Matthew has some important lessons on prayer, including the Lord's Prayer.[Mt.6:5-15]

There are times when you should join with other Christians in united prayer.[Mt.18:19-20] The early Christians *all continued with one accord in prayer and supplication.*[Ac.1:14; Ac.2:42-47; Ac.4:24]

In some way, at some time, at some place, develop the habit of praying every day. Do not just say words. A good practice is to ask only for something that you do expect to receive. God wills to answer prayer.

This is the confidence that we have in him, that, if we ask anything according to his will (His word or His promises which are written so that we can know His will), *he hears us: and if we know that he hears us, whatever we ask, we know that we have the petitions that we desired of him.*[1Jn.5:14-15]

You will come against obstacles in prayer. People and the devil will try to discourage you. But when you pray, believe you receive what you ask for and it will come to you.[Mk.11:24]

Claim the answer and *fight the good fight of faith.*[1Ti.6:12] Believe for an answer because of 1) the promises of God, 2) the power of the name of Jesus and 3) the power of the Holy Spirit. You and God are able to work wonders together. You, with God, are a majority over the devil. *All things are possible to those who believe.*[Mk.9:23]

Discover the thrill of putting God's word to the test and of seeing it fulfilled.

Practice every day, talking to God.

Chapter 6

How God Talks to You

LET GOD TALK to you every day.

This is what happens when you read the Bible.

When you open the Bible and read it, you are hearing God talk.

Prayer and reading of the Bible should always go together. One is not complete without the other. By prayer, you speak to God. When you read the Bible, God speaks to you. There is no real communion or communication unless you both take part in the conversation.

Many years ago, when my wife and I were first married, we were pastors of a church. We always spent two or three hours of each day in prayer.

Often I prayed in the basement of our house.

God used an older Christian to help us learn many lessons. He visited us occasionally to share some good thought about a verse of scripture. He gave us valuable counsel as young ministers.

One day he came while I was praying. My wife, Daisy, did not disturb me, so he waited for a while, then left. The next day he came back. I was praying again in the basement. He could hear me. The third day it happened again.

Finally he left a message with Daisy:

"Tell Pastor Osborn that God is very polite; as long as he does all the talking, God won't interrupt." I got the point, and learned a vital lesson about communion with God.

Let God talk to you each day. Read His word.

Prayer is a two-way conversation. You talk to Him and then you listen while He talks to you.

Jesus said, *You shall not live by bread alone, but by every word that proceeds out of the mouth of God.*[Mt.4:4]

The word of God is food for your soul.

Job said, *I have esteemed the words of his mouth more than my necessary food.*[Jb.23:12]

As newborn babes, desire the sincere milk of the word, that you may grow thereby.[1Pe.2:2]

You nourish your physical body with natural food two or three times a day.

Nourish your soul with spiritual food at least once every day.

Your words were found, and I did eat them; and your word was the joy and rejoicing of my heart.[Je.15:16]

The law of the Lord is perfect, converting the soul: the testimony of the Lord is sure, making wise the simple. The statutes of the Lord are right, rejoicing the heart: the commandment of the Lord is pure, enlightening the eyes; more to be desired are they than gold, yes, than much fine gold: sweeter also than honey and the honeycomb.[Ps.19:7-10] So, every day let God speak to you, through reading His word. Accept what it says. God says what He means. He needs no interpreter. He is a masterful communicator.

The New Testament was written originally in common, not classical Greek so that the common people[Mk.12:37] could understand its important message.

A. Read it because it is food for your soul.

B. Read it because it is a guide for your feet.

Your word is a lamp to my feet, and a light to my path.[Ps.119:105] *The commandments of the Lord are pure, enlightening the eyes.*[Ps.19:8]

The entrance of your word gives light; it gives understanding to the simple.[Ps.119:130]

For the commandment is a lamp; and the law is light; and reproofs of instruction are the way of life.[Pr.6:23]

C. Read it because it is your spiritual weapon.

Take the sword of the Spirit, which is the word of God.[Ep.6:17] *For the word of God is quick, and powerful, and sharper than any twoedged sword.*[He.4:12]

Therefore shall you lay up these my words in your heart and in your soul, and bind them for a sign upon your hand, that they may be as frontlets between your eyes.[De.11:18]

D. Read it because it has a purifying power.

How shall the youth cleanse their way? By taking heed according to your word.[Ps.119:9]

Now you are clean, Jesus said, through the word which I have spoken to you.[Jn.15:3] *Sanctify them through your truth: your word is truth.*[Jn.17:17]

E. Read it because it has converting power.

The law of the Lord is perfect, converting the soul.[Ps.19:7]

Being born again, not of corruptible seed, but of incorruptible seed, by the word of God, which lives and abides forever.[1Pe.1:23]

I am not ashamed of the gospel of Christ: for it is the power of God to salvation to every one that believes.[Ro.1:16]

The holy scriptures are able to make you wise to salvation through faith which is in Christ Jesus.[2Ti.3:15]

F. Read it because it has healing power.

God sent his word and healed them, and delivered them from their destruction.[Ps.107:20]

And it came to pass on a certain day, as Jesus was teaching, the power of the Lord was present to heal the people.[Lu.5:17]

Jesus cast out the spirits with his word, and healed

all that were sick.[Mt.8:16]

G. Read it because it is so profitable.

Lay up these words in your heart. Teach them to your children, speaking of them when you sit in your house, and when you walk by the way, when you lie down, and when you rise up. Write them upon the door posts of your house, and upon your gates.[De.11:18-20]

All scripture is given by inspiration of God, and is profitable for doctrine, for reproof, for correction, for instruction in righteousness. That the child of God may be perfect, thoroughly furnished to all good works.[2Ti.3:16-17]

H. Read it because it rejoices the heart.

The statutes of the Lord are right, rejoicing the heart.[Ps.19:8]

Let the word of Christ dwell in you richly in all wisdom; teaching and admonishing one another in psalms and hymns and spiritual songs, singing with grace in your hearts to the Lord.[Co.3:16]

I. Read it to keep from error and sin.

You err, not knowing the scriptures.[Mt.22:29]

Your word have I hid in my heart that I might not sin against you.[Ps.119:11]

J. Read it because we are told to do so.

And it shall be with you, and you shall read therein all the days of your life: that you may learn to fear the Lord your God, to keep all the words of this law and these statutes, and do them.[De.17:19]

Seek out the book of the Lord, and read: not one of these shall fail.[Is.34:16]

Search the scriptures; they testify of me.[Jn.5:39]

Study to show yourself approved by God, a witness that needs not be ashamed, rightly dividing the word of God.[2Ti.2:15]

K. Read it because it is enduring.

For ever, O Lord, your word is settled in heaven.[Ps.119:89]

Concerning your testimonies, I have known of old that you have founded them for ever.[Ps.119:152]

The grass withers, the flower fades: but the word of our God shall stand for ever.[Is.40:8]

For verily I say to you, Till heaven and earth pass, one jot or one tittle shall in no wise pass from the law, till all be fulfilled.[Mt.5:18]

But the word of the Lord endures for ever.[1Pe.1:25]

John saw a vision. *He was called Faithful and True. And he was clothed in a vesture dipped in blood; and his name is called The Word of God.*[Re.19:11,13]

So read the Bible every day and let God talk to you through it.

Jesus said, *Heaven and earth shall pass away, but my words shall never pass away.*[Mt.24:35]

Balaam said, *God is not a man, that he should lie;*

neither the son of man, that he should repent: has he said, and shall he not do it? or has he spoken, and shall he not make it good? [Nu.23:19]

Solomon said, *There has not failed one word of all his good promises.* [1K.8:56]

David said, *For ever, O Lord, your word is settled in heaven.* [Ps.119:89]

God said to Jeremiah, *I will hasten* (watch over, protect, stand behind, enforce) *my word to perform it.* [Je.1:12]

God told Isaiah, *My word that goes forth from my mouth: it shall not return to me void, but it shall accomplish that which I please, and it shall prosper in the thing whereto I sent it.* [Is.55:11]

God said to Ezekiel, *For I am the Lord: I will speak, and the word that I shall speak shall come to pass.* [Eze.12:25]

Chapter 7

How to Share the Good Life

TALK TO SOMEONE else about God every day.

That is witnessing of Christ to others.

The Bible says: *This is a faithful saying, and worthy of all acceptation, that Christ Jesus came into the world to save sinners.*[1Ti.1:15]

The Son of man is come to seek and to save that which was lost.[Lu.19:10]

Jesus came to save sinners. That was His mission.

First and last, Jesus was a soulwinner — the greatest soulwinner the world has ever known.

The first group He chose to follow Him received this challenge: *Come after me, and I will make you to become fishers of mankind.*[Mk.1:17]

The last group who followed Him out to His ascension received this command: *Go make disciples of all nations.*[Mt.28:19 RV]

First and foremost, Jesus was a soulwinner. That is what He came for, *to save sinners.* That is what He lived for — and died for — and rose again for — and sent back the Holy Ghost to His followers for — to make them effective soulwinners.

And He said to his disciples, *as my Father sent me, even so send I you,*[Jn.20:21] and then and there *He breathed on them and said, Receive the Holy Ghost.*[Jn.20:22] What for? *And you shall receive power after that the Holy Ghost is come upon you: and you shall be witnesses to me.*[Ac.1:8]

That is the mission — the ministry of every Christian, to tell others the good news.

Paul said, *The same good news that came to you is going out all over the world and changing lives everywhere, just as it changed yours that very first day you heard about God's great kindness to sinners.*[Co.1:6 LB] He talked about *the great love for others which the Holy Spirit has given to us,*[Co.1:8 LB] then added: *So everywhere we go we talk about Christ to all who will listen* (because) *this is our work, and we can do it only because Christ's mighty energy is at work within us.*[Co.1:28-29 LB]

The Bible says that the early Christians were *daily in the temple and in every house, and they ceased not to teach and preach Jesus Christ,*[Ac.5:42] *and the word of God increased and the number of disciples multiplied greatly.*[Ac.6:7]

You see, there are just two basic principles involved in the good life.

1) Your faith.

2) Your ministry.

First: What you believe.

Second: What you do and say as a result.

You are saved to save others.

For with the heart you believe to righteousness, and with the mouth confession is made to salvation.[Ro.10:10]

If you believe on Jesus Christ, you want to talk about Him to others. That is witnessing.

Your faith is what you believe.

Your ministry is what you say and do about it.

Has Jesus Christ done something so good for you that you cannot keep quiet about it?

In Bible days, the people were always so grateful for what the Lord had done for them that they rushed about, telling it to everyone else who would listen.

Did you ever stop to think about this: The word Christian means Christlike.

Since Christ came to save sinners, to seek out the lost, then to be like Christ — Christian, we are to be soulwinners. If Christ is born in us, He wills to do the same things in and through us as He did when He walked on earth.

Yet there are hundreds of thousands of professing Christians who have never known the joy of letting Christ win a soul through them. There are preachers and priests who have never won a soul.

Jesus took His message to the sinners; to the marketplaces, to street corners, to the mountainsides, to the seashores, to the homes of sinners.

They criticized Him by accusing: *This man receives sinners, and eats with them.*[Lu.15:2]

He mixed with sinners, witnessed to them, convinced them and won them. He was not a holier-than-thou type, aloof, superspiritual, self-righteous. He walked with sinners. They were His reason for being in this world.

So it is with every true Christian. To be Christ-like means to win souls. His purpose is our purpose. His mission is our mission. His plan is our plan. He came to save sinners. We are to be like Him. We are here, in this world, for the same purpose.

He said: *I came into the world, that I should bear witness to the truth.*[Jn.18:37] That is why we are in this world — to bear witness of the gospel to others who do not know Christ as Savior and Lord.

He commanded: *Go out into the highways and hedges, and compel them to come in, that my house may be filled.*[Lu.14:23]

Every follower of His did just that.

After His ascension, His early followers acted

just like Him. Every one of them was busy witnessing. Each believer was a witness. They were busy in the markets, in the streets, in houses, around the public wells, talking, reasoning, witnessing, convincing, preaching, winning souls, compelling sinners to believe the gospel – just like Jesus did.[Ac.5:42]

In fact, they reminded everyone so much of Christ, that critics, with contempt in their voices, sarcastically called them Christians.[Ac.11:26] They were called fanatics because they were like Christ in witnessing to others.[Ac.8:4]

Jesus was *moved with compassion* [Mt.9:36] when He saw the people without faith and hope. When we are like Christ, we are moved with that same compassion.[2Co.5:14] We simply cannot keep quiet about what Christ has done for us. So as Paul said, *Everywhere we go we talk about Christ to all who will listen* because *this is our work.*[Co.1:28-29 LB]

Talk to someone else about Christ each day. Do not let a day go by that you do not share the good news with somebody.

My book, *Soulwinning,* will be very helpful to you. It is considered a classic on this very important subject. Get copies for your pastor, Bible teacher, for a missionary or some Christian friend. Its influence is proven and many souls will be saved as a result of your sharing this book with others.

The late Dr. Harry Denman said: "Unless Christians catch the vision of personal soulwinning, the world will be lost."

Billy Graham says: "The greatest need in the world today is for the sharing of the gospel with individuals — not by the professional clergy, but by ordinary Christians."

When Paul spoke about the real Christian, he spoke of a ministry: *If you are in Christ you are a new creature and God* (has) *both reconciled you to himself by Jesus Christ, and has given you the ministry of reconciliation.*[2Co.5:17-18]

Any one who is in Christ, is a new creature and has received a ministry of reconciliation. Every Christian has a ministry of reconciling people to God through Christ. That is soulwinning — regardless of color, race, nationality or sex. Every believer is a proclaimer. Every receiver is a sharer. Every Christian is a missionary — an evangelist — a witness. This is Christianity in depth.

That is why I say, talk to someone else about God every day. It is the ministry nearest the heart of God. It is why Christ died. It is why He shed His blood. It is the last thing Jesus told us to do. It is the reason for being empowered by the Holy Spirit. It is the purpose of a Christian's life.

When I say to the wicked, you shall surely die; and you give no warning, nor speak to warn the wicked from their wicked way, to save their lives; the same wicked person shall die in iniquity; but their blood will I require at your hand.[Ez.3:18]

It is a Christian's highest opportunity in life – to share the good news of Jesus Christ with others. It would be dreadfully selfish to know about Christ and what He did to save sinners; to receive Him and His peace, then to remain silent before others. We shall not keep quiet. We shall share the good news.

That is witnessing for Christ.

Christianity has been carried down through these twenty centuries by ordinary lay people who have been constrained by the love of Christ [2Co.5:14] to tell others about His mercy and salvation. Tens of thousands of them have been persecuted, tortured and even martyred as the seed of the church.

When others have paid such a supreme price to bring us the gospel, we cannot keep it to ourselves. We share it with others. This is the essence of Christianity in action.

You need not be a Bible student or be eloquent of speech. Talk to people about Christ, like you talk to them about any other friend.

If you know John 3:16 and a few verses in Romans, that is enough. Five simple facts are sufficient to bring anyone to a decision for Christ.

1. PEOPLE'S NEED — Romans 3:23.

2. SIN'S PENALTY — Romans 6:23a.

3. CHRIST'S REMEDY — Romans 5:8.

4. GOD'S GIFT TO PEOPLE — Romans 6:23b.

5. HOW TO RECEIVE — Romans 10:9-10,13.

You can mark these verses in the margin of your New Testament as a chain of references to follow in each conversation. They constitute the ROMAN ROAD that leads to Christ.

Here is a convenient outline to help you show anyone the way to God's goodness and to guide you if you personally need His salvation:

FIRST: THE PRINCIPLE OF SELF-VALUE

You are created in God's image to share His life, love, plan and purpose and you are therefore, infinitely valuable to Him.

For you are God's workmanship.[Ep.2:10]

God created mankind in his own image, in the image of God created he him, male and female created he them.[Ge.1:27]

The Lord made people a little lower than God, and crowned them with glory and honor. The lord gave them dominion over the works of his hands; he put all things under their feet.[Ps.8:5-6]

SECOND: THE BASIC PROBLEM IN LIFE

Adam and Eve chose not to trust God's word.

And the Lord God told (Adam and Eve), *Of every tree of the garden you may freely eat; but of the tree of the knowledge of good and evil, you shall not eat of it; for in the day that you eat of it you will surely die.*[Ge.2:16-17]

Satan influenced them to distrust God's word. He contradicted God by saying: *You will not surely die.*[Ge.3:4]

Eve took of the fruit and ate it, and gave some to her husband with her; and he ate it.[Ge.3:6]

That was the original sin — distrusting God's word.

THIRD: THE NEGATIVE POWER OF UNBELIEF

To question God's integrity produces deterioration and death in human nature.

God said, In the day that you refuse my instructions and eat the fruit I forbade, you will surely die.[Ge.2:16-17]

The wages of sin (disregarding the integrity of God's word) is death.[Ro.6:23]

Whereas, by one person sin entered into the world, and death by sin; so death passed upon all persons, for that all have sinned.[Ro.5:12]

FOURTH: THE LOVE-PLAN OF GOD

God loved and valued you too much to let you die. He gave Jesus to be judged and condemned in your place, to release you from all guilt.

God was not willing that any should perish, but that all should come to repentance.[2Pe.3:9]

God so loved the world that he gave his only begotten Son, that whoever believes in him will not perish, but have everlasting life.[Jn.3:16]

But God showed his great love for you by sending Christ to die for you.[Ro.5:8 LB]

Now God says he will accept and acquit you – declare you not guilty – if you trust Jesus Christ to take away your sins. For God sent Christ Jesus to take the punishment for your sins and to end all God's anger against you. Your acquittal is not based on your good deeds; it is based on what Christ has done and your faith in him.[Ro.3:22,25,27 LB]

Because no debt can be paid twice, or no crime punished twice, you can be restored as though you had never done wrong.

Since Jesus Christ suffered the penalty you deserved, and since He did it on your behalf, you are no longer guilty before God and need never be judged for any sin you have ever committed.

The judgment you deserved was put on your substitute, in your place, and that judgment can never be imposed on you again.

That was God's love plan to save you and restore you to the life and goodness for which He originally designed you.

FIFTH: THE SECRET OF IDENTITY WITH CHRIST

You are restored to God's life again when you receive Jesus Christ.

When you identify with what Jesus Christ did, and believe that He assumed all judgment for your sins in your place, this is what takes place:

1) The righteousness of Christ is transferred to you and you are free of all guilt and judgment. 2) Jesus Christ comes and lives the life of God in and through you. 3) You become a new creation. 4) You are restored to God according to His original plan. 5) A supernatural power is given to you which makes you a child of God. This is a miracle.

God made Jesus Christ who knew no sin to be made sin on our behalf, so that in him we might share the righteousness (or life) *of God.*[2Co.5:21]

As many as receive Jesus Christ, God gives them power to become a child of God.[Jn.1:12]

If you are in Christ, you are a new creature. All things become new.[2Co.5:17]

Jesus said, *I am come that you might have life more abundantly.*[Jn.10:10]

You are restored to friendship, fellowship and life with God when you receive Christ. And that is the way you were designed to live.

Truly your fellowship is with the Father, and with his Son Jesus Christ.[1Jn.1:3]

When anyone accepts Christ, even the simplest prayer is enough. The man in the Bible prayed: *God be merciful to me a sinner.*[Lu.18:13] The thief on the cross prayed: *Lord, remember me when you come into your kingdom.*[Lu.23:42] It is enough to pray:

Dear Lord:

I confess that I did not trust Your word.

I call upon Your name.

Forgive all of my sins.

I believe You died in my place.

I accept You as my personal Savior.

I believe You rose from the dead according to the scriptures.

I receive You and Your life from God.

I believe You do save me now.

Thank You, Jesus, for my salvation.

Amen.

MAKE your motto in life the same as ours: ONE WAY! ONE JOB!

The **One Way** is Jesus.[Jn.14:6]

The **One Job** is to witness of Him to others.[Is.43:10; Jn.15:27; Ac.1:8; Ac.2:32; Ac.5:42; Ac.22:15; Ac.28:31]

It is the work nearest the heart of God and your

life will be as blessed as Jesus' life was blessed because *as the Father sent him into the world, even so he has sent you into the world,*[Jn.17:18] and He promises, *Lo, I am with you, alway, even to the end of the world.*[Mt.28:20]

When I was only a lad and received Jesus into my life, I started telling others about Him. I had a small toy press. I took bits of paper, and printed a message on each one, which included John 3:16.

Then I delivered those little tracts door-to-door in the town where I lived.

Who could ever have dreamed that we would publish over a ton of gospel literature every day in over 132 languages?

When you are consistent and speak to someone every day about Christ, you will be amazed at how God will enlarge your daily capacity.

Let your creed be: Every Christian a witness.

Let your mission be: Out where the people are.

I heard the voice of the Lord, saying, Whom shall I send, and who will go for us? Then said I, Here am I; send me.[Is.6:8]

Lift up your eyes, and look on the fields; for they are white already to harvest.[Jn.4:35]

Jesus said, *The harvest truly is plenteous, but the labourers are few.*[Mt.9:37]

Jesus Christ died for the whole world. His

blood was shed for the remission of sin. He did this for every person on earth who will call on Him. But *how shall they call on him in whom they have not believed? And how shall they believe in him of whom they have not heard?* [Ro.10:13-14]

So then faith (for salvation) *comes by hearing the word of God.* [Ro.10:17]

You and I are the witnesses, the confessors, the testifiers, the voices, the preachers, the instruments through which this world must hear the gospel. Christ lives and ministers through us.

This is the last thing Jesus commanded us to do. [Mt.28:19-20] This was not a suggestion. This was a commission.

This is why I say to develop the habit of talking to someone else about God every day, and you will always be a happy, successful, vibrant Christian. You will know how to really live the good life.

Chapter 8

A Certain Neighbor

A CERTAIN MAN moved into our community; he didn't fall among robbers, who stripped him and beat him, leaving him half dead. He just moved in. And by chance a certain neighbor was going down that way; and when he saw him, he passed by on the other side, saying to himself, "I am almost late now for the meeting at the church. If I stop to visit, I will surely miss the opening prayer. Besides, the church probably knows about him."

And in like manner also another neighbor came to the place and saw him, passed by on the other side, saying, "So they want us to visit new neighbors such as this one? Well, I do not believe in giving the impression that I am a fanatic on religion. I will just wait until he casually speaks to me some day, and then I will say, `Pardon me, don't think I am the type who goes overboard on such things, but if you ever get a chance you might like to visit our church when you feel like it and the children are not sick and you do not plan to go out of town, or have guests, and you have the time."

But a certain neighbor on a journey, came where he was, and seeing him, was moved with compassion, and came to him and welcomed him to the community, and invited him to church, and even offered to come by for him. The following Sunday the believer brought the new neighbor to the pastor and said, "Take care of him, and if I can be of further service, I will be glad to do it."

Which of these three, do you think, proved neighbor to the newcomer in the community?

Chapter 9

Russian Famine

DURING THE YEARS 1920 and 1921, it is estimated that nearly 20 million people starved to death in the great Russian famine. A man in America sent funds every month to his brother in Russia to sustain him and his three sisters.

After the famine, the brother came to the United States and it was learned that he was the only family survivor — the others had starved.

One day the American brother said: "George, how did it happen? Did not I send you enough?"

George made nervous and incoherent excuses.

Eight months later George was dying. His guilt gave him no peace. He called his brother: "Peter, there was enough, but I kept it for myself." Then he died.

Suppose that was our attitude about the bread of life at the end of the way?

There was enough for every creature, but we kept it for ourselves — and the others starved.

Only three percent of all the souls born this year will hear the gospel.

There is enough. Are we just keeping it for ourselves?

In our crusades I meet thousands of Christians who have a zeal to give the bread of life to others. They believe I have been successful in doing this. They ask me for the secrets. As I have shared these secrets, other Christians have become fruitful soulwinners. I believe the greatest privilege of every Christian is to be a witness for Christ.

Chapter 10

Man from Australia

DID YOU EVER save anyone from perishing? Were you ever in a situation where you were the only one who could save a person's life?

I saved a boy from drowning one time. I was standing on the shore of a lake when I saw the lad struggling far out in the water. He had dived off his boat and had been swimming out in the deep water, then he swam toward his boat to rest. But he did not see that the wind had caught his boat and was moving it faster than he could swim. The boy could never reach the shore; I knew he would drown unless something was done quickly.

There was a canoe nearby. I grabbed it with one hand, and a broken oar with the other. I rushed into the water and rescued him just before he drowned. When I brought him to shore, I thanked God that I had been able to reach him before he perished.

As I looked at him, safe and sound, I do not think I ever felt better in my life. I had saved a boy from perishing. Some day I will stand on the shores of heaven. I will get to look at the redeemed souls I have been able to reach with the gospel. I will listen to them sing. I will rejoice that I was able to reach them before they perished. Their presence in heaven with me will be the greatest reward I can imagine.

Years ago a man was leaving Australia after making a fortune in the gold mines. The ship on which he was sailing was broken in the storm and it began to sink. The lifeboats were lost and the people were without hope. This man thought he could fight through the waves and reach a small island nearby.

He was about to leap into the water when a small girl whose mother had been lost in the sea clutched his clothes in fear. She begged, "Mister, please can you save me?"

Around his waist he had buckled a heavy belt of gold which was his fortune. He looked back at the helpless girl. He had to choose between his worldly fortune and the girl's life.

As the winds beat the salt water in his face and the girl clung to him, he unbuckled the heavy belt of gold and threw it into the water. Then he grasped the little girl and flung himself overboard. He struggled every yard of the way through the turbulent waters.

Finally, with life almost gone, he reached the land. As he staggered to the shore and placed the girl safely on the sand, he sank in exhaustion and became unconscious.

Later when consciousness returned to him the little girl put her arms around his neck and her lips to his cheek. She looked at him with her soft eyes and said, "Mister, I'm so glad you saved me. Thank you for what you did."

The man said that was worth more to him than all the gold of Australia.

When we reach the glittering shores of heaven, let us make sure there will be souls who will run to greet us with outstretched arms and say, "Welcome! Welcome! I am so glad you made it possible for me to be saved!"

PART

III

SECRETS OF SUCCESS

WHY DOES each person have special abilities to do certain things best? Why do some people abandon all hope of ever getting good things from God?

There are just seven basic needs in each life. There is a simple secret to receiving health, happiness, success and prosperity. There is an abundance of all of it, and it is for you.

When you discover your roots with God, you will find a gold mine for yourself and for your loved ones. ➡

Chapter 11

How to Develop Success and Happiness

IN ADDITION TO the three daily Christian habits of 1) prayer, 2) Bible reading and 3) witnessing, here are some further secrets of success for the good life.

In the third century, Cyprian, the Bishop of Carthage, wrote to his friend Donatus: "It is a bad world, Donatus, an incredibly bad world. But I have discovered in the midst of it a quiet and holy people who have learned a great secret. They have found a joy which is a thousand times better than any of the pleasures of our sinful life. They are despised and persecuted, but they do not care. They are masters of their souls. They have overcome the world. These people, Donatus, are Christians and I am one of them."

If you have repented of your sins and have received Christ as Savior, then you, too, are one of them.

A vital step in your following Christ is your fellowship with other Christians.

The Bible teaches that *You are the body of Christ,*

and members in particular; [1Co.12:27] That all believers are to *become more and more in every way like Christ who is the head of his body, the church. Under his direction the whole body is fitted together perfectly, and each part in its own special way helps the other parts, so that the whole body is healthy and growing and full of love.* [Ep.4:15-16 LB]

Paul says of individual Christians: *Some of us have been given special ability as apostles; to others Christ has given the gift of being able to preach well; some have special ability in winning people to Christ, helping them to trust him as their Savior; still others have a gift for caring for God's people as a shepherd does his sheep, leading and teaching them in the ways of God.*

Why is it he gives us these special abilities to do certain things best? It is that God's people will be equipped to do better work for him, building up the church, the body of Christ, to a position of strength and maturity; until finally we all believe alike about our salvation and about our Savior, God's Son, and all become full-grown in the Lord – yes, to the point of being filled full with Christ. [Ep.4:11-13 LB]

We will lovingly follow the truth at all times – speaking truly, living truly – and so become more and more like Christ who is the head of his body, the church. [Ep.4:15 LB]

And now you have become living building-stones for God's use in building his house. What's more, you are his holy priests; so come to him – (you who are acceptable to him because of Jesus Christ) – and offer to God those things that please him.[1Pe.2:5 LB]

And so, I plead with you to give your bodies to God. Let them be a living sacrifice, holy – the kind he can accept. When you think of what he has done for you, is this too much to ask?

Don't copy the behavior and customs of this world, but be a new and different person with a fresh newness in all you do and think.

Then you will learn from your own experience how his ways will really satisfy you.[Ro.12:1-2 LB]

Be honest in your estimate of yourselves, measuring your value by how much faith God has given you.

Just as there are many parts to our bodies, so it is with Christ's body. We are all parts of it, and it takes every one of us to make it complete, for we each have different work to do.

So we belong to each other, and each needs all the others.

God has given each of us the ability to do certain things well.

So if God has given you the ability to prophesy, then prophesy whenever you can – as often as your faith is strong enough to receive a message from God.

If your gift is that of serving others, serve them well.

If you are a teacher, do a good job of teaching.

If you are a preacher, see to it that your sermons are strong and helpful.

If God has given you money, be generous in helping others with it.

If God has given you administrative ability and put you in charge of the work of others, take the responsibility seriously.

Those who offer comfort to the sorrowing should do so with Christian cheer.

Don't just pretend that you love others: really love them.

Hate what is wrong.

Stand on the side of the good.

Love each other with brotherly and sisterly affection and take delight in honoring each other.

Never be lazy in your work, but serve the Lord enthusiastically.

Be glad for all God is planning for you.

Be patient in trouble, and prayerful always.

When God's children are in need, you be the one to help them out.

And get in the habit of inviting guests home for dinner or, if they need lodging, for the night.

If people mistreat you because you are a Christian, don't curse them; pray that God will bless them.

When others are happy, be happy with them. If they

are sad, share their sorrow.

Work happily together. Don't try to act big. Don't try to get into the good graces of important people, but enjoy the company of ordinary folks. And don't think you know it all.

Never pay back evil for evil. Do things in such a way that everyone can see you are honest clear through.

Don't quarrel with anyone. Be at peace with everyone, just as much as possible.

Dear friends, never avenge yourselves. Leave that to God, for he has said that he will repay those who deserve it. (Don't take the law into your own hands.)

Instead, feed your enemy that is hungry. If thirsty give something to drink and you will be "heaping coals of fire on their head." In other words, they will feel ashamed for what they have done to you.

Don't let evil get the upper hand but conquer evil by doing good.[Ro.12:3-21 LB]

Obey the government, for God is the one who has put it there. Obey the laws.[Ro.13:1-5 LB]

Pay your taxes too for government workers need to be paid so that they can keep on doing God's work, serving you.[Ro.13:6 LB]

Pay everyone whatever is due them; pay your taxes and import duties gladly, obey those over you, and give honor and respect to all those to whom it is due.

Pay all your debts except the debt of love for others

– never finish paying that!

If you love your neighbor as much as you love yourself you will not want to harm, or cheat, or kill, or steal from them. And you won't sin with the spouse or want what is theirs, or do anything else the Ten Commandments say is wrong.[Ro.13:7-9 LB]

Another reason for right living is this: you know how late it is; time is running out. Wake up, for the coming of the Lord is nearer now than when we first believed.

The night is far gone, the day of his return will soon be here. So quit the evil deeds of darkness and put on the armor of right living, as we who live in the daylight should!

Be decent and true in everything you do so that all can approve your behavior.

Don't spend time in wild parties and getting drunk or in adultery and lust, or fighting, or jealousy.

But ask the Lord Jesus Christ to help you live as you should, and don't make plans to enjoy evil.[Ro.13:11-14 LB]

Give a warm welcome to any person who wants to join you, even though their faith is weak. Don't criticize them for having different ideas from yours.[Ro.14:1 LB]

God has accepted them to be his children. They are God's servants, not yours. They are responsible to him, not to you. Let him tell them whether they are right or wrong. And God is able to make them do as they should.[Ro.14:3-4 LB]

You have no right to criticize others or look down on them. Remember, each of us will stand personally before the Judgment Seat of God. Yes, each of us will give account to God.

So don't criticize each other any more. Try instead to live in such a way that you will never make another person stumble by letting them see you doing something they think is wrong.[Ro.14:10-13 LB]

Don't do anything that will cause criticism against yourself even though you know that what you do is right. For, after all, the important thing for us as Christians is not what we eat or drink but stirring up goodness and peace and joy from the Holy Spirit.

If you let Christ be Lord in these affairs, God will be glad; and so will others. In this way aim for harmony in the church and try to build each other up.[Ro.14:16-19 LB]

May God who gives patience, steadiness, and encouragement help you to live in complete harmony with each other – each with the attitude of Christ toward the other.

And then all of us can praise the Lord together with one voice, giving glory to God, the Father of our Lord Jesus Christ.

So, warmly welcome each other into the church, just as Christ has warmly welcomed you; then God will be glorified.[Ro.15:5-7 LB]

I commit you to God, who is able to make you strong and steady in the Lord, just as the gospel says, and just as I have told you.

This is God's plan of salvation. This message is being preached everywhere, so that people all around the world will have faith in Christ and obey him. To God, who alone is wise, be the glory forever through Jesus Christ our Lord. Amen.

Sincerely,

Paul Ro.16:25-27 LB

Chapter 12

How to Pray and Get an Answer

THERE IS NO greater secret to the good life than to learn to pray and to get an answer. God wants you, as His child to come to Him with absolute confidence that whatever you need or desire, you can ask Him for it in simple prayer and faith, and it shall be done for you.

He made many marvelous promises – and they are for you – personally:

Call to me, and I will answer you, and show you great and mighty things which you know not.[Je.33:3]

This is God's invitation to prayer and His promise to answer.

Ask, and it shall be given you; seek, and you shall find; knock, and it shall be opened to you.[Mt.7:7]

This is Christ's encouragement to prayer and His assurance that your prayers will be answered.

Everyone that asks receives.[Mt.7:8]

This is His promise that everyone in a million who asks shall receive. In His mind, there is no such thing as unanswered prayer.

The one that seeks finds.[Mt.7:8]

To the one that knocks it shall be opened.[Mt.7:8]

It is always His will to answer prayer. That is His delight.

God invites you to pray — to ask. He is always ready to answer you.

When people do not pray, it is because they have no hope of an answer.

Unanswered prayers stand between people and their faith.

Some say: "I could have faith but I have prayed so many prayers and never received an answer." Or they say: "I used to have faith until I prayed so desperately about a particular problem, and the answer never came."

Many people blame God for unfaithfulness when they should blame themselves for not praying according to His word.

Usually people do not accuse God of failing to do His part, but they harbor an inner confusion — a bewildered attitude toward prayer which has developed from repeatedly failing to get the answer. They have inwardly abandoned the hope of receiving what they ask for, so they abandon prayer altogether.

This amounts to a surrender of faith.

People who do not pray are disappointed in their faith. Their hopes for an answer have been shattered too often. They have given up. Now they continue only in the formality of religion. Reality has ceased to exist.

When faith's light has gone out, life becomes a tedious road.

Abandon faith and you walk life's road alone, for God cannot keep company with unbelief.

Fear and insecurity enslave the life where faith has been surrendered.

You need not lose hope and conclude that prayer is useless.

You can pray and receive the answer.

One of the most marvelous communions any person can enjoy with the Lord is *to ask and to receive.*[Mt.7:8]

It is wonderful, indeed, that those who have perhaps only received an answer to their prayers once in a lifetime, remember that experience the rest of their life.

An old gentleman must dry the tears from his eyes as he relates the one time in his life, perhaps years ago, when he cried out to God in a desperate time and God heard his prayer and answered.

Yet our heavenly Father invites us to enjoy this blessing every day of our lives.

You can enjoy this joyous privilege today, and every day, throughout the rest of your life.

Release and forget those unanswered prayers which are stacked away in the seclusion of your memory.

Let go of the past. Do you feel that you failed? Never mind. A host of other people have done the same thing. A host of them also surrendered their future with those past failures.

However, there is another group who, by an act of their own will, wrote those memories off as bad accounts and began life anew. They succeeded. They found happiness and God's abundance as well.

The foundation for answered prayer is to realize that the only reason you can expect any blessing from God is that Jesus died to provide that blessing.

You see, thousands of people pray but never stop to see if what they ask for is provided by Christ's death.

They want healing "because they have suffered so much," or "because they have been a good, sincere person," or "because they have been faithful to the church," or for some similar reason.

Is this logic a basis for receiving healing from Christ?

I believe that our real foundation for healing by

faith is: *Himself took our infirmities, and bore our sicknesses.*[Mt.8:17] *Certainly he carried our diseases and suffered our pains; and with his stripes we are healed.*[Is.53:4-5]

To get your prayers answered, depend entirely on the merits and mediation of Jesus Christ.

Whatever you pray for, understand that Christ died to provide it at the cross.

In His death for us, Christ provided every blessing that can be desired or required.

When you pray, look first to the cross where the price was paid for the blessing you seek.

Understand that since Christ died to provide the blessing, it belongs to you and He wants you to have it. Therefore, claim it, boldly.

Your needs are sevenfold. Seven is the perfect, complete number in the Bible. God reveals Himself by seven redemptive names, showing His sevenfold nature which imparts His sevenfold blessing to our lives when we receive Him. Christ's death paid the full price for this sevenfold redemption. Everything we can require or desire Jesus provided at the cross.

In the Scofield Bible, page 7, item (4) under the commentary on Genesis 2:4, the Seven Redemptive Names of Jehovah are outlined.

Jehovah-tsidkenu, God is our RIGHTEOUSNESS.[Je.23:6]

Jehovah-Shalom, God is our PEACE.[Jdg.6:23-24]

Jehovah-raah, God is our GUIDE or SHEPHERD.[Ps.23:1]

Jehovah-rapha, God is our PHYSICIAN or HEALER.[Ex.15:26]

Jehovah-jireh, God is our PROVIDER or SOURCE.[Ge.22:8-14]

Jehovah-shammah, God is EVER PRESENT.[Ez.48:35]

Jehovah-nissi, God is our VICTORY.[Ex.17:15]

These seven names reveal God's nature to mankind. Being redemptive names, they reveal the redemptive blessings which He wills for everyone. There are no exceptions in Christ's redemptive work. God's redemptive will is proven by Christ's death on the cross. All of this means that every blessing provided by the death of Christ on the cross is included in our redemption, and there can be no exceptions. They are all for *whoever will.*

The very foundation for receiving answers to your prayers is to base your faith on the fact that Christ died to provide that for which you are asking.

You do not claim healing because you have been good, or faithful to church, or because you have suffered too long, or because your family needs you, or because you want to work for Him.

There is only one reason for claiming health from God: *Christ bore your diseases and suffered your pains and by his stripes your healing was provided freely.*[Is.53:4-5]

This is a legal basis for your claim. You are God's child. He provided your health by submitting to and enduring your diseases. He wants you to be well. Health, therefore, belongs to you. It is paid for and is offered freely. You have a legal right to this blessing. It awaits your claim just like an amount of money deposited to your account at the bank.

The fact that Christ died to provide your health makes it unnecessary for you to suffer disease. It makes it unjust and illegal for Satan to impose disease on your body. He has no right to inflict your body with what God laid on Jesus for you. Resist the oppressor steadfastly in faith.[1Pe.5:9] Claim your health on the basis of Christ's bearing away your diseases.[Mt.8:17] Refuse to bear the curse of sickness because Christ was made a curse for you and took your sicknesses.[Ga.3:13]

See your healing as a part of your redemption. Understand that health has been deposited to your account. Above all, realize that Christ suffered so that you might be made whole.

Sickness is of the devil.[Jb.2:7; Lu.13:11,16; Ac.10:38] It is a curse.[De.28:15-18; Ga.3:13] It is not natural. It is a killer. It came because Adam and Eve sinned in the garden of Eden. Disease never came from God. Satan brought it.

When God redeemed us, the salvation provided by Christ included deliverance from sin and its effects. Sickness is part of the effect of sin in the human race.[Ps.103:3]

When Christ bore our sins and put them away,[1Pe.2:24] He also bore our sicknesses and put them away.[Is.53:4-5] He suffered in our stead. He redeemed us. He set us free by bearing the punishment we merited.[Ro.5:8; Ro.6:6]

We deserved to die in our sins. Christ died in our place, being made sin for us.[2Co.5:21]

We were entitled to suffer disease. Christ carried our diseases and suffered our pains for us, and *by his stripes we were healed.*[Is.53:4-5]

Make Christ's death your only argument — the only basis for claiming any blessing.

When He paid such an enormous price to provide the blessings and gifts you need, no other point is worthy of mentioning before Him.

Your needs are sevenfold. God's nature is sevenfold. Christ's provision is sevenfold. Redemption is sevenfold.

Let us look at God's sevenfold full life policy. Let us see what you have claim to.

1. YOU NEED FORGIVENESS and righteousness because you feel condemnation. Sins loom up before you. They haunt you every time you need God's help and accuse you of unworthiness. You falter and waver every time the devil passes them across your mind. They hinder you every time you think of praying. You have become desperate. You must have them out of the way forever. You want His righteousness, His forgiveness; you want the question of your sins settled forever.

PROVISION: Christ *his own self bore our sins in his own body on the tree, that we, being dead to sins, should live unto righteousness.*[1Pe.2:24] God *made him* (Christ) *who knew no sin to become sin for us, that we might be made the righteousness of God in him.*[2Co.5:21] *The Lord* (is) *our righteousness.*[Je.23:6] Jesus became your righteousness by bearing your sins on the cross; therefore, *the gift of righteousness*[Ro.5:17] is yours now; Jesus paid for it. Your sins can no longer condemn you, for Christ put them away forever. Satan has no right to accuse you by reminding you of them in your times of crisis, for they are carried away as far as the east is removed from the west.[Ps.103:12] They are gone. Christ paid for every one of them. The penalty has been suffered. The payment has been made. You are free.[Jn.8:36]

BASIS FOR FAITH: Christ was made sin with your sins and bore the punishment which you deserved. That is the only reason you can claim exemption or forgiveness for your sins and live free from condemnation.

PRAYER – When you seek forgiveness or righteousness.

Lord, I understand that Jesus took my sins to the cross; His blood was shed for their remission; I confess and forsake them. I am forgiven. Christ suffered my penalty. I am saved. He gives me His righteousness. I accept it as a free gift by faith. I am free from my sins. They are paid for. Christ took them to the cross.

2. YOU NEED PEACE. Your soul is in turmoil. You feel uneasy and tense, accused and condemned. You need things settled in your soul. You are restless and tormented. You need peace.

PROVISION: The Lord is our peace.[Jdg.6:20-24] Jesus says: *My peace I give to you.*[Jn.14:27] This is yours. Jesus died to provide it because *the chastisement of our peace was upon him*[Is.53:5] when He *made peace through the blood of his cross.*[Co.1:20] Satan has no right to rob you of this heritage. Christ died under the anguish of your sins that you might have his peace.

BASIS FOR FAITH: Christ endured the cross, bearing your chastisement to give you peace. That is the only reason you can claim His peace and refuse all inner conflict.

PRAYER – When you seek His peace:

Lord, You bore my chastisement and made peace by the blood of the cross; I claim Your peace in my soul. Nothing can upset, condemn or accuse me because when Your blood was shed, my sins were removed forever and no longer can enmity exist between us. I claim that peace now. It is mine. The conflict ended at the cross. My account was settled. Now I have Your peace forever.

3. YOU NEED GUIDANCE. You think you might be deceived so you are troubled and cautious, fearful and hesitating. You are asking for His guidance, but you are not sure. You waver. You need Him to lead you.

PROVISION: *The steps of good people are ordered by the Lord.*[Ps.37:23] *Your word is a lamp to my feet, and a light to my path.*[Ps.119:105] *The Lord is my shepherd.*[Ps.23:1] Jesus said: *My sheep hear my voice, and they follow me; a stranger they will not follow.*[Jn.10:27, 5] He has become your guide. You can be sure. He paid for the privilege of leading you by giving *his life for the sheep.*[Jn.10:11] His death opened the way for you to belong to Him and to follow Him.

BASIS FOR FAITH: Christ gave His life to become your shepherd. That is the only reason you can claim His guidance and be assured that you will never go, or be led astray.

PRAYER – When you seek His guidance:

Lord, You are my shepherd. I follow You. I

know Your voice. You gave Your life for me. I can never be misled for I have You as my guiding shepherd.

4. YOU NEED HEALING. You are suffering from pain or disease, weakness or sickness. You are in desperate need of God's healing power. You are praying for deliverance.

PROVISION: Christ paid for your perfect and complete healing when He died on the cross. He is the *Lord that heals you.*[Ex.15:26] He *heals all your diseases.*[Ps.103:3] He paid for your healing when He *carried your diseases and suffered your pains, taking the stripes by which you were healed.*[Is.53:4-5] It is finished now.[Jn.19:30] Your health is paid for. Your diseases were laid on Him; He took them away forever. Healing belongs to you now. It is a gift. It is yours. Satan has no right to lay on you what God laid on Jesus at the cross.

BASIS FOR FAITH: Christ suffered your diseases and carried them for you in His death. That is the only reason perfect healing belongs to you and you have a right to claim health in His name.

PRAYER – When you seek healing:

Lord, You laid my diseases and my pains on Jesus and He carried them away for me in His death. Since He suffered them for me, I need never suffer them. I am free. I am healed. I count the scriptures true which say that He bore them for me. I claim my health now.

5. YOU ARE IN NEED. You face impossibilities. You are desperate. The devil torments you. You cry and beg. You fear. You are asking God to supply because He alone is your source.

PROVISION: *My God shall supply all your needs according to his riches in glory by Christ Jesus.*[Ph.4:19] God reveals Himself as the great provider and in a type of Calvary, He promised to Abraham: *The Lord will provide.*[Ge.22:8] He did provide everything you could require or desire when at the cross He provided complete redemption. Since Christ died for you, *how shall he not with him also freely give us all things?*[Ro.8:32] *All (things) are yours; and you are Christ's and Christ is God's.*[1Co.3:22-23]

BASIS FOR FAITH: Christ emptied himself on the altar of the cross to give you all God possesses. That is the only reason He supplies all of your needs and you need never suffer the fear of lack.

PRAYER – When you are in need:

Lord, You gave Jesus to die in my stead. His death made me Your child. When You gave Jesus for me, You also freely gave me all things. All you have is, therefore, mine. I claim what my present needs require, because Jesus died so I could enjoy fullness and plenty.

6. YOU NEED GOD'S PRESENCE. You are lonely. You feel far from God. You need Him with you. You feel helpless and insecure. You need the friend who is closer than a brother or sister.

PROVISION: *The Lord is there* (or present).[Ez.48:35] He says: *I will never leave you, nor forsake you.*[He.13:5] This blessing is provided through Christ's death for we were *made nigh by the blood of Christ.*[Ep.2:13] It is He who left us with His promise: *Lo, I am with you always.*[Mt.28:20]

BASIS FOR FAITH: Christ shed His blood to bring you to God. That is the only reason you can claim God's presence with you and be assured that you are never alone or helpless. He is your friend. Christ made you nigh to Him. He is there.

PRAYER – When you ask for His presence:

Lord, I know that Christ made me nigh to You by His blood. He put away all of my sins. Therefore I can rest secure with Your presence near me. His blood is the proof that I am nigh to You. I depend on Your presence for You are with me always. I am not alone. You are by my side.

7. YOU NEED VICTORY. You are in a battle. You are fighting the enemy. You falter under his blows and you fear defeat. You are praying desperately for help from the Lord. You need victory in your battle.

PROVISION: *The Lord is our banner* or victor or captain.[Ex.17:15 LB] It was when Christ triumphed over principalities and powers,[Co.2:15] that He provided for us the privilege of shouting: *Thanks be to God, who gives us the victory through our Lord Jesus Christ.*[1Co.15:57] His death conquered every foe. He has delivered you from the power of darkness, and has translated you into the kingdom of His dear Son.[Co.1:13] His death signaled your eternal victory. Satan will never challenge the cross. He was defeated there.

BASIS FOR FAITH: Christ died to conquer Satan and to triumph over his kingdom of demons. That is the only reason you need never fear demons and you can claim victory in every battle.

PRAYER – When you seek victory:

Lord, I know that Jesus triumphed over Satan and all principalities. He arose the Victor. His victory is my victory. I claim my rights. I stand by faith. I raise my hands in triumph. My battle was won at the cross. I have no fear. I rest in His triumph. Satan was defeated. Christ is the winner. My battle is over. Jesus is Lord!

THE GREATEST TRAGEDY among Christians today is that people do not understand the substitutionary fact of Christ's death.

He did not die for Himself. He died for you.

He did not carry His own sin away. He never sinned. He put your sin away.

He did not conquer and triumph over Satan for

Himself. He did it for you.

He did not shed His blood so that He could be near God. You are made nigh by the blood of the cross.

He did not empty Himself on the altar of the cross to supply His own needs. He did it for you so that you could enjoy all God possesses and never suffer lack.

He did not have disease of His own. He took your diseases away and healed you.

The cross is not heaven's triumph over Satan. It is your triumph over Satan.

God did not need victory over Satan. You had sinned, you needed redemption. In order for God to deal justly with Satan and provide you a just redemption, He gave His Son and required that He suffer all of the punishment you deserved; all of the consequences Satan intended to pour out on his new slave the human race. Jesus took that all on Himself, for you. Then, triumphantly, you were raised with Him.[Co.2:12-13; Co.3:1-2] His victory was for you. You are now redeemed. You are free from sin. You are the conqueror. You have peace now. You have no lack now. You are healed now.

When you approach God in prayer, do not come as a beggar. You are His child.

You will not receive these blessings Christ died to provide if you ignore the cross and His suffering which paid for them.

That is why I impress upon you: The foundation for answered prayer is to realize that the only reason you can expect any blessing from God is that Jesus died to provide that blessing.

Since it is provided in His death, then it is yours.

Chapter 13

How to Practice the Presence of Jesus

SINCE YOU HAVE received Christ and He has come to live in you,[Jn.14:23] begin to practice being conscious of His presence with you and in you. It is when He becomes a real partner with you that you begin to live the good life.

You yielded your life to Jesus Christ. You know He is in you and with you.

For you are dead, and your life is hid with Christ in God,[Co.3:3] *for Christ is our life.*[Co.3:4] So recognize His presence in four distinct ways.

THINK NOTHING that you would not think if you could actually sense the thinking process of Christ at work within your mind.

For to be carnally minded is death, because the carnal mind is enmity against God for it is not subject to the law of God, neither indeed can be.[Ro.8:6-7]

Be not conformed to this world, but be transformed by the renewing of your mind, that you may prove what is that good, and acceptable and perfect will of God.[Ro.12:2]

Be renewed in the spirit of your mind; and put on the new creation, which is created in righteousness and true holiness.[Ep.4:23]

Let this mind be in you which was also in Christ Jesus.[Ph.2:5]

Whatever things are true, whatever is honest, whatever is just, whatever is of good report; if there be any virtue, and if there be any praise, think on these things,[Ph.4:8] *because we have the mind of Christ.*[1Co.2:16]

SAY NOTHING that you would not like for Jesus Christ to hear you say.

In the sight of God, we speak in Christ.[2Co.2:17]

David said, *I will speak of your testimonies. I will not be ashamed.*[Ps.119:46] *My tongue shall speak of your word.*[Ps.119:172] *My mouth shall speak the praise of the Lord.*[Ps.145:21]

Paul said, *It is written, I believed, and therefore I have spoken: we also believe, and therefore we speak.*[2Co.4:13]

We learn to believe God's word so much that we use it when we speak. *The word is near you, even in your mouth, and in your heart: that is the word of faith, which we preach* (or speak).[Ro.10:8] That is why *they overcame him* (the accuser) *by the word* (they spoke in) *their testimony.*[Re.12:11]

Jesus said, *For out of the abundance of the heart the mouth speaks. A good person out of the good treasure of the heart brings forth good things; and an evil per-*

son out of the evil treasure of the heart brings forth evil things. But I say to you, that every idle word that you shall speak, you shall give account thereof in the day of judgment. For by your words you shall be justified, and by your words you shall be condemned.[Mt.12:34-37] (Be sure to study chapters 14 and 15 of this book.)

So, *only let your conversation be as it becomes the gospel of Christ,*[Ph.1:27] and say only what agrees with the word of God. Be conscious of Christ's presence in everything you say. He is there. Let Him speak through you.

Let your speech be always with grace, seasoned with salt, that you may know how you should answer everyone.[Co.4:6] Use *sound speech that cannot be condemned.*[Ti.2:8]

Jesus said, *Whoever confesses me before people, I will confess before my Father which is in heaven.*[Mt.10:32]

GO NO PLACE where Jesus Christ cannot be welcomed as your companion.

Christ has become an integral part of your life. He says, *Lo, I am with you alway.*[Mt.28:20] *I will dwell in them, and walk in them; and I will be their God, and they shall be my people.*[2Co.6:16] Therefore, do not embarrass your Lord. He loves you and cherishes your company. He says: *If you love me and keep my words, my Father and I will come to you, and live with you.*[Jn.14:23]

Set your affection on things above, not on things on

the earth. For you are dead, and your life is hid with Christ in God, for Christ is our life.[Co.3:2-4]

Wherefore come out from among them, and you be separate, says the Lord, and touch not the unclean thing; and I will receive you. Having therefore these promises, dearly beloved, let us cleanse ourselves from all filthiness of the flesh and spirit, perfecting holiness in the fear of God.[2Co.6:17; 2Co.7:1]

And you, being in time past alienated and enemies in your mind in your evil works, yet now has he reconciled in the body of his flesh through death, to present you holy and without blemish and unreprovable before him: if so be that you continue in the faith, grounded and steadfast, are not moved away from the hope of the gospel which you heard.[Co.1:21-23 RV]

The Lord has promised to be *a very present help in trouble* [Ps.46:1] and to *never leave you nor forsake you,*[He.13:5] so never go any place where your Lord Jesus cannot accompany you or where you would not want Him to see you.

He is *a friend that sticks closer than a brother or sister* [Pr.18:24] and He wanted your companionship enough to die for your sins so He could redeem you back into His fellowship. So only go where you can be proud to invite Him along as your best friend.

DO NOTHING that you would not do if you could see Christ bodily looking on.

For the grace of God that brings salvation has appeared to all, teaching us that, denying ungodliness and worldly lusts, we should live soberly, righteously, and godly in this present world; looking for that blessed hope, and the glorious appearing of the great God and our Savior Jesus Christ; who gave himself for us, that he might redeem us from all iniquity, and purify to himself a peculiar people, zealous of good works.[Ti.2:11-14]

Be ready for every good work.[Ti.3:1] *I will that you which have believed in God might be careful to maintain good works. These things are good and profitable.*[Ti.3:8] *That you might show forth the praises of him who has called you out of darkness into his marvelous light.*[1Pe.2:9]

Be rich in good works.[1Ti.6:18]

In all things show yourself as a pattern of good works.[Ti.2:7]

God is able to make all grace abound toward you; that you always having all sufficiency in all things, may abound to every good work.[2Co.9:8] Paul prayed *that the child of God may be perfect, throughly furnished to all good works,*[2Ti.3:17] and urged every believer to *purge yourself from* (dishonorable things, so that you can) *be a vessel to honor, sanctified, and meet for the master's use, and prepared for every good work,*[2Ti.2:20-21] because He said, the seal of the foundation of the Lord is: *The Lord knows them that are his. And, let everyone that names the name of*

Christ depart from iniquity.[2Ti.2:19]

For it is written, As I live, says the Lord, every knee shall bow to me, and every tongue shall confess to God. So then every one of us shall give an account of ourselves to God.[Ro.14:11-12]

When Christ actually lives in you, then He expresses His life through you. Your body is His temple.[1Co.6:19] His mind becomes yours.[1Co.2:16] His love is manifested through you. His emotions and affections become yours.[2Co.5:14] All this happens to you as you learn to *put on the Lord Jesus Christ.*[Ro.13:14; Ga.3:27] The result is that *He works in you both to will and to do his good pleasure.*[Ph.2:13]

So as you grow in the good life, you train yourself to practice the presence of Jesus Christ in you and with you in these basic ways:

1. You **think** as Jesus would think through you.

2. You **speak** as Jesus would speak with your lips.

3. You **go** where Jesus can go with you.

4. You **do** as Jesus does through you.

Jesus is present in your life every moment. Since you are His body, He wants to express Himself and carry out His mission of love to others through you. Practice letting Him do it.

Once I saw a picture of Christ with one hand lifted toward heaven and the other reaching down toward people in need who were gathered about Him. That is the way it is. We learn that just as Jesus Christ is God's bridge to humanity, we now become His bridge to them, because *in him we live, and move, and have our being* [Ac.17:28] and He uses our faculties to express Himself to people. We let Him use our hands and bodies to achieve His purpose.

He has no hands but our hands
To do His work today.
He has no feet but our feet
To lead us on His way.
He has no tongue but our tongue
To tell the world He died.
He has no help but our help
To bring them to His side.

PART

IV

GOOD LANGUAGE FOR GOOD LIVING

YOUR THOUGHTS ARE the seeds of your life. Your words are your method of planting those seeds.

Your words establish your standard of living.

Your life will always be at the level of your conversation.

You always talk what you really believe.

With your words, you constantly paint a public picture of your own inner self.

You can discover how to talk yourself to the top and win with God. ➠

Chapter 14

How to Talk Yourself to the Top

NOTHING IS MORE important in living the good life than to learn the good language.

Christianity is also called confession.[He.10:23 RV]

Paul emphasized two essentials in our "profession" or "confession": 1) What we believe: *For with the heart you believe to righteousness,* and 2) What we say about it: *With the mouth, confession is made to salvation.*[Ro.10:10]

Jesus confessed who He was. We are to confess who we are in Him. We are constantly to believe and confess:

That we are redeemed.[Re.5:9; 1Pe.1:18]

That we are born again.[Jn.1:12-13; Jn.3:7; 1Pe.1:23]

That we have a new nature.[2Co.5:17; Ga.6:15; Ep.4:22-24; Co.3:9-10]

That our redemption is a fact.[Ep.1:7; Co.1:14; He.9:12]

That we are healed.[Is.53:4-5; 1Pe.2:24; Ex.15:26]

That all our needs are supplied.[Ph.4:19; Ps.84:11; 2Co.9:8]

That we are not afraid.[Jos.1:9; Ps.27:1,3; Ps.23:4; Ps.56:11;

Ps.91:1-7,9-12; Is.41:10

That Christ lives in us.[*2Co.6:16; Jn.14:23; Ga.2:20; Jn.17:23; Co.1:27*]

That He is our strength, our provider, our healer, our keeper.[*Ph.4:13; Ps.31:19; Ex.15:26; 2Ti.1:12; 2Th.3:3; Jude 24*]

That we are delivered out of Satan's power.[*Co.1:12-14; Jb.5:19; Da.6:27; 2Co.1:10*]

That we are partakers of the new nature.[*2Pe.1:4; 1Co.10:16-17; Co.1:12; He.3:14*]

That we have the righteousness of Jesus.[*Ro.5:17; Ph.3:9; 1Co.1:30*]

That we are no longer condemned.[*Ro.8:1; Jn.5:24*]

That we are justified.[*Ro.5:1,18; Ga.3:24*]

That we are more than conquerors.[*Ro.8:37*]

That we are no longer under Satan's dominion.[*Co.1:12-14; Lu.10:19*]

That defeat and failure are things of the past.[*Ep.2:1-6; 2Co.5:17*]

That we are linked up with God.[*Ep.2:6; Co.2:9-10*]

That He is our partner and companion and friend in life.[*Pr.18:24; Jn.15:13-16; Jn.17:21-23*]

That we are saved.[*Ac.2:21; Ep.2:8; 2Ti.1:9; Ti.3:5*]

That we have the good life.[*Jn.10:10; 2Pe.1:3-4*]

In these next two chapters, you will find scripture references to support every one of these confessions. Learn them; mark them in your Bible and make them part of your conversation.

Thousands of Christians live far below their privileges in Christ and constantly negate the good life by retaining their old confessions. Your words control and dominate you, because they express your thoughts which are the seeds of your life.

Learn to think the good life, and talk or confess the good life. Sooner than you ever dreamed, your actions will express your thoughts and words and you will live the good life.

Always, the process is: 1) THOUGHTS, 2) WORDS, then 3) DEEDS.

Now that you have been born again, never think or talk on the level of the old life. *Old things are passed away.*[2Co.5:17] Change your thoughts and words.[Is.55:7-8]

If you will observe closely, you will notice that every time you allow yourself to think negatively and to speak negatively, you act negatively.

You said you did not have faith, and at that moment, doubt arose like a giant and bound you.

Perhaps you never realized that you are ruled by your words.

Solomon said, *You are snared with the words of your mouth, you are taken* (captive) *with the words of your mouth.*[Pr.6:2]

You talked failure, and failure held you in bondage.

You talked fear, and fear increased its grip on you.

First we fill our hearts with the word of God. Then we confess that word until it becomes a part of our nature.

Our hearts and our lips harmonize with the Father's word.

David realized this when he prayed: *Set a watch, O Lord, before my mouth; keep the door of my lips.*[Ps.141:3]

Let the words of my mouth, and the meditation of my heart, be acceptable in your sight, O Lord, my strength and my redeemer.[Ps.19:14]

Those who overcome the devil, do so *by the blood of the Lamb, and by the word of their testimony;*[Re.12:11] that is, the scriptures they quote as they give their testimony.

Have you ever noticed what John said? *For this purpose the Son of God was manifested, that he might destroy the works of the devil.*[1Jn.3:8] *Having spoiled principalities and powers, he made a show of them openly, triumphing over them in it.*[Co.2:15]

According to these scriptures, Jesus has destroyed the works of the devil, spoiled his power, and triumphed over him. Since Satan's works have been destroyed, his power has been spoiled, and he has been triumphed over, he must be a defeated foe.

Jesus' triumph was our triumph. His victory was our victory. He did nothing for Himself. He did it all for us. He defeated Satan for us. He destroyed the works of the devil for us. He conquered Satan for us.

All that Jesus did was for us and we are now partakers of his victory.[Ep.2:5-6; Co.1:12-14]

We were captives, but Christ has freed us from captivity.[Jn.8:32; Ro.6:22]

We were cursed by sin and sickness, but Christ, our Redeemer, has freed us from that curse, and loosed us from its dominion.[Ga.3:13]

We were weak, but the Lord has become our strength, so now we are strong.[Ps.27:1; Ps.28:7; Jl.3:10; 2Co.12:10]

We were bound and imprisoned, but Christ has freed us from slavery.[Jn.8:36; Ro.8:2]

We were sick, but Christ has borne our sicknesses and carried them away, so now *with his stripes we are healed.*[Is.53:5; 1Pe.2:24]

Confess that you are the conqueror.[Ro.8:37] *Then hold fast your confession of faith without wavering, (for He is faithful that promised).*[He.10:23 RV]

When Jesus arose from the dead, He left an eternally defeated Satan behind Him. Always think of Satan as eternally defeated. Think of Satan as one over whom Jesus, and you in Jesus' name, have entire dominion and authority.[Ep.1:19-23; Ph.2:9-11]

These are facts which are eternal. Confess them boldly. Stand on them.

Simply to admire these facts in the Bible and to say that you believe them, but never to confess them boldly and act on them, robs you of faith in the time of need.

We know that Christ put Satan and all his kingdom beneath our feet, and that we are considered by the Father and by Satan as victors. We have been liberated. Our language becomes like that of superhuman beings. We talk as if we are people of another kingdom, and that we are: *A chosen generation, a royal priesthood.*[1Pe.2:9] We have authority. God is supporting our position. We are bold. We speak God's language as commonly as the unbeliever talks his fears.

We confess what we are in Christ. We confess that we are redeemed, that our redemption is an actual fact; that we are delivered out of the dominion and authority of Satan. We confess these facts boldly, with absolute certainty, because we know they are true.

We confess that we are new creatures [2Co.5:17]

recreated in Christ Jesus — that we are partakers of his divine nature.[2Pe.1:4]

We confess that sickness, disease, fear, weakness, and failure are things of the past.

A wrong confession is the confession of defeat, failure, and of the supremacy of Satan. Talking about your combat with the devil, how he has hindered you, and how he is holding you in bondage, oppressing you with problems, and keeping you sick is a confession of defeat.

As long as you hold fast to the confession of weakness, poverty, sickness and defeat, you will continue to have them. You may search for years for some servant of God to pray the prayer of faith for you, but it will be of no avail, because your unbelief will destroy the effects of faith.

Every time you confess weakness and failure, you magnify the adversary above the Father. You thus destroy your own confidence in God's word. Study the Bible until you know what your rights and privileges are. Then *hold fast your confession.*[He.10:23 RV]

Confess the work Christ finished. Confess the authority He gave you over Satan. *Behold, I give you power over all the power of the enemy, and nothing shall by any means hurt you.*[Lu.10:19]

Confess your supremacy over the devil. Believe that you are more than a conqueror over him. He knows that he cannot rule you any longer. Believe God's word. Be bold in its truth. Confess only what God says. Keep that confession. Don't change it. Let God's word *live in you,* and you *live in it.*[Jn.15:7-8]

Take this sample scripture: *Therefore if any one be in Christ, he or she is a new creature.*[2Co.5:17]

That does not mean that we are just forgiven sinners — poor, weak, staggering, sinning church members. That means that we are new creatures now. We have been created in Christ Jesus, with the life of God, the nature of God, and the ability of God within us. Confess that.

Old things are passed away; behold, all things are become new.[2Co.5:17] Confess it. Believe it. It means we are new. All things are new. Old things are gone. Those old earmarks of sin, sickness, disease, failure, weakness and fear have all passed away. Now we have God's nature, his life, his strength, his health, his glory, his power. We have it now.

Let this scripture become a reality: *Fear not; for I am with you: be not dismayed; for I am your God: I will strengthen you; I will help you; I will uphold you with the right hand of my righteousness.* [Is.41:10]

If God be for us, who can be against us? [Ro.8:31]

Such scriptures as these must be your confession as you stand before the world.

You are of God, little children, and have overcome

them: because greater is he that is in you, than he that is in the world.[1Jn.4:4]

You face life fearlessly. You know now that greater is He that is in you, than all the forces that can be arrayed against you.

You are filled with joy and victory because God has taken over your problems.

You are not afraid of circumstances, because you *can do all things through Christ which strengthens you.*[Ph.4:13] He is not only your strength, but He is by your side. He is your salvation. Whom should you fear? [Ps.27:1] He throws light on life's problems so that you can act intelligently. He is your salvation and deliverance from every trap that the enemy sets for you – from every snare in which he would enslave you.

The Lord is the strength of (your) *life; of whom shall* (you) *be afraid?* [Ps.27:1]

You are not afraid of anything. You have no fear because God is on your side. This is your confession.

Hold fast the confession of your faith without wavering, (for he is faithful that promised.) [He.10:23 RV]

Remember, you were a slave of Satan. You were bound by sin and sin's penalty. You were subject to Satan's authority. But now you are free.

The Spirit of the Lord is on me. He has anointed me to preach the good news; to tell the prisoners they are free; to tell captives they are released.[Is.61:1]

Confess your freedom. Believe in your freedom. Your redemption is a fact. Act on your liberty. Your full pardon has been granted. Your prison is open. Your bondage is past. What God says is yours. Believe it. Confess it. Act on it.

Chapter 15

The Wonder of Saying What God Says

REMEMBER THAT YOUR faith can never rise higher than your confession. The promises of God become real and living only as we confess them. To enjoy the good life, you must learn the value of God's word on your lips.

You cannot talk contrary to God's word and win His blessings.

Your words are your standard of faith. They express what you really believe.

Did you realize that multitudes of people fail in life because they talk failure? They fear failure. They really believe in failure.

Your life will always go to the level of your words.

This is one of the simplest facts of life, yet the principle is practiced by only a few. That is why only a small number of people are really successful.

They practice talking defeat and thinking defeat, then they fail.

The Bible has much to say about your words. It constantly warns against negativism and unbelief. It abounds with exciting examples of those who speak faith.

When you talk right, you train yourself to think right and to act right.

Remember this fact: You will not — you cannot — rise above your own words. If you talk defeat, fear, failure, anxiety, sickness, unbelief, you will live on that level. You, nor anyone else, will ever live above the standard of your conversation. This principle is unalterable.

If conversation is foolish, trifling, impractical and disorganized, life is invariably the same way.

With your words, you constantly paint a public picture of your inner self.

Jesus said: *Out of the abundance of the heart, the mouth speaks.*[Mt.12:34]

You talk what you believe. If your talk is careless, negative or confusing, it is because your heart is that way.

If you talk disease, fear, anxiety and frustration, your words are painting the true picture of what you really believe.

If your heart and mind are filled with God's word, you will talk that word.

Your confession is your real faith talking.

There is no believing that does not express itself in confession.

Jesus demanded that you not only believe on Him but that you confess Him before people.[Mt.10:32]

You have a right to say what God says.

If God has said it in His word, then you can confess it, knowing that God will make it good.

That is what is meant by this verse: *For He has said, I will never leave you, nor forsake you. So that we may boldly say, the Lord is my helper.*[He.13:5-6]

It is because of what *He has said* that we may speak boldly.

Because He has said, *The Lord has pleasure in the prosperity of his servants,*[Ps.35:27] and *wealth and riches shall be in his house,*[Ps.112:1,3] we may boldly say, "Yes, Lord, You take pleasure in blessing me with plenty. You are the source of all wealth and riches and You do will them for my house."

Because He has said, *I am the Lord that heals you,*[Ex.15:26] we may boldly say, "Yes, Lord, You are the Lord Who heals me."

Let no thought dwell in your mind that contradicts what He has said. You boldly say and think the same things.

Instead of fearing disease or being frustrated by the threat of illness, boldly say, "The Lord heals me." Believe it. Read it. Ponder it until your heart overflows with it. Your faith will confess it boldly. You are sure. God confirms it.

Because He has said, *With his stripes we are healed,*[Is.53:5; 1Pe.2:24] we may boldly say, "Yes, Lord, with Your stripes I am healed now."

Meditate on it. Let your heart overflow with it. Confess it boldly. Act on it. Because God said it, you may boldly say it and God will make it so.

God says of His own word: *For I am the Lord: I will speak, and the word that I shall speak shall come to pass. The word which I have spoken shall be done, says the Lord God.*[Ez.12:25,28]

You can count on God's word being good. It cannot fail because God cannot fail.

The word is God speaking. It reveals the mind and will of God. It is alive. It abides forever. It shall never pass away. It is a part of God himself. God cannot fail, so His word cannot fail.

Jesus said, *The scripture cannot be broken.*[Jn.10:35]

God said, *My word that goes forth out of my mouth shall not return to me void, but it shall accomplish the thing whereto I sent it.*[Is.55:11]

Because God has spoken, therefore we may boldly say the same thing, and be absolutely certain that we shall have it.

Because He has said, *I am come that they might*

have life, and that they might have it more abundantly,[Jn.10:10] we may boldly say, "I have that abundant life dwelling in me now, because I have received Jesus Christ."

Because He has said, *Seek first the expansion of God's kingdom worldwide and all these things shall be added to you,*[Mt.6:33 RV] we may boldly say, "Everything I need in life is mine, from Christ, because I am involved in God's No. 1 Job of soulwinning."

Because He has said, *If God be for us, who can be against us?* [Ro.8:31] we may boldly say, "God is for me and no one can succeed against me."

Because He has said, *Beloved, I wish above all things that you may prosper and be in health, even as your soul prospers,*[3Jn.2] we may boldly say, "I have a right to prosperity and health, because I am prospering in my soul."

Because He has said, *Fear not; for I am with you: be not dismayed; for I am your God,*[Is.41:10] we may boldly say, "I am no longer afraid because God is with me now all the time."

Because He has said, *The Lord shall command the blessing on all that you set your hand to, and he shall make you plenteous in goods,*[De.28:8,11] we may boldly say, "God is blessing what I do and I shall succeed and prosper in whatever I put my hand to, because God cannot fail to back up His word."

Because He has said, *You shall know the truth,*

and the truth shall make you free,[Jn.8:32] we may boldly say, "I am set free, for I know His blessed truth."

Because He has said, *Let the weak say, I am strong,*[Jl.3:10] we may boldly say, "I can do all things through Christ which strengthens me."[Ph.4:13]

Because He has said, *My God shall supply all your need according to his riches in glory by Christ Jesus,*[Ph.4:19] we may boldly say, "God knows every need I face and He is now supplying for those needs, and my supply is as unlimited as the riches of Christ Jesus."

Because He has said, *Resist the devil, and he will flee from you,*[Ja.4:7] we may boldly say, "The devil is fleeing from me, for I am steadfastly resisting him in Jesus' name."

Because He has said, *Himself took our infirmities, and bore our sicknesses,*[Mt.8:17] we may boldly say, "I am free from weakness and disease because they were all carried by Jesus Christ for me."

Because He has said, *Whoever shall confess me before others, I will confess before my Father,*[Mt.10:32] we may boldly say, "Jesus is confessing me right now to the Father because I am confessing Him before people."

Because He has said, *He that raised up Christ from the dead shall also quicken your mortal bodies by his Spirit that dwells in you,*[Ro.8:11] we may boldly say, "God is quickening my mortal body now by the very same Spirit that raised Jesus from the dead, because His Spirit dwells in me; thus I am free from weakness and sickness."

Because He has said, *They that seek the Lord shall not want any good thing,*[Ps.34:10] we may boldly say, "God cannot allow me to lack any good thing. He takes care of my every need, because I do seek Him with all my heart."

Because He has said, *God has not given us the spirit of fear; but of power, and of love, and of a sound mind,*[2Ti.1:7] we may boldly say, "I am free from all fear, for my God has given me power, love and a sound mind."

Because He has said, *Give, and it shall be given to you; good measure, pressed down and running over,*[Lu.6:38] we may boldly say, "The Lord is heaping up my blessings, for I am giving to Him and to His work."

Because He has said, *They shall lay hands on the sick, and they shall recover,*[Mk.16:18] we may boldly say, when we lay hands on the sick, "They are recovering because I am acting on God's word."

Because He has said, *In my name they shall cast out devils,*[Mk.16:17] we may boldly say, "Devils are going out because I have commanded them to go, in Jesus' name."

Because He has said, *When the enemy shall come*

in like a flood, the Spirit of the Lord shall lift up a standard against him,[Is.59:19] we may boldly say, "God's Spirit is raising a mighty standard of defense in my behalf at the very time the enemy is heaping his pressure on me. Praise the Lord, my case is in His hands."

Because He has said, *Your God whom you serve continually, He will deliver you,*[Da.6:16] we may boldly say, "God is my deliverer in every case, because I constantly serve Him."

Because He has said, *Blessed be the Lord who daily loads us with benefits,*[Ps.68:19] we may boldly say, "I praise You, Lord, because You are filling my life with Your abundance of blessings and good things."

Because He has said, *The Lord is nigh to all them that call on him in truth,*[Ps.145:18] we may boldly say, "The Lord is near to me now, because I call on Him."

Because He has said, *The Lord shall fight for you, and you shall hold your peace,*[Ex.14:14] we may boldly say, "I know God is fighting for me because I am holding my peace. I have committed my battle into His hands."

Because He has said, *I can do all things through Christ which strengthens me,*[Ph.4:13] we may boldly say, "Nothing is impossible for the Lord and me, because He lives in me and it is He who is doing the work even now.

Because He has said, *You shall serve the Lord, your God, and he shall bless your bread, and your water; and I will take sickness away from the midst of you,*[Ex.23:25] we may boldly say, "Sickness is taken away from me; my bread and my water are blessed, because I am serving the Lord my God."

Because He has said, *Before they call, I will answer; and while they are yet speaking, I will hear,*[Is.65:24] we may boldly say, "The Lord is answering my prayer even now as I pray; in fact He was already working on the answer before I prayed."

Because He has said, *In all these things we are more than conquerors through him that loved us,*[Ro.8:37] we may boldly say, "I am a conqueror; I am a winner, because Christ who loved me is in me now and no evil can defeat Him who lives in me."

Because He has said, *Jesus Christ the same yesterday, and to day, and for ever,*[He.13:8] we may boldly say, "The Lord will do as much for me today as He ever did for anyone else, because He is unchanged."

Because He has said, *Go your way and as you have believed, so be it done to you,*[Mt.8:13] we may boldly say, "I can be on my way; I have prayed and believed; the answer will come just as I am expecting."

Because He has said, *There is therefore now no condemnation to them which are in Christ Jesus,*[Ro.8:1] we may boldly say, "I am forever free from all guilt and condemnation before God because I am living in Christ Jesus now."

Make God's word the standard for your life. Train yourself to say what He says. Sooner than you can imagine, your life will rise to the level of His word in your heart and on your lips.

God is in His word. When you confess it, He makes it good. You become the master of every situation because God is on your side. You are aligning yourself on the side of His word. He takes your part, to confirm His word, and your enemy goes down in defeat.

Because He has said, *I will never leave you, nor forsake you,* we may boldly say, "The Lord is my helper." [He.13:5-6] For *If God be for us, who can be against us?* [Ro.8:31]

Because He has spoken, we know we can declare it boldly. It will be as He has said, because *There has not failed one word of all his good promise which he promised.* [1K.8:56]

"Listen to me, and you will have a LONG, GOOD LIFE. Carry out my instructions, for they will lead you to REAL LIVING." Prov. 4:10,13 Living Bible

"How excellent is your lovingkindness, O God! ... (to those who) put their trust under your wings. They shall be abundantly satisfied, they shall drink of the river of YOUR pleasure. For with YOU is the fountain of LIFE." Psalm 36:7-9

Discover HIS *Good Life.* Live in harmony with God. Get His ideas. Work with His projects. See LIFE as He sees it. Discover who YOU are and YOUR own value. See yourself as God sees you. Live interested in His plans. He believes in YOU and treasures YOUR companionship.

For more than a half century, T.L. and Daisy Osborn have shared with multitudes of people in 73 nations, the principles of *The Good Life* which God created humanity for. It is believed that the two of them, as messengers of *Good News*, have proclaimed the gospel of Jesus Christ to more *non*-Christians, and have seen a greater number of conversions, than any other couple in the world. Every outreach of their world ministries addresses women and men *equally*, and emphasizes the *Good News* that Christ has come so *"that YOU may have LIFE — more abundantly."* John 10:10

OSBORN CRUSADE Ponce, Puerto Rico

OSBORN CRUSADE Lubumbashi, Zaire

OSBORN CRUSADE Cabanatuan, Luzon

OSBORN CRUSADE Kampala, Uganda

OSBORN CRUSADE Madurai, India

OSBORN CRUSADE Lagos, Nigeria

OSBORN CRUSADE Djakarta, Java

OSBORN CRUSADE San Fernando, Trinidad

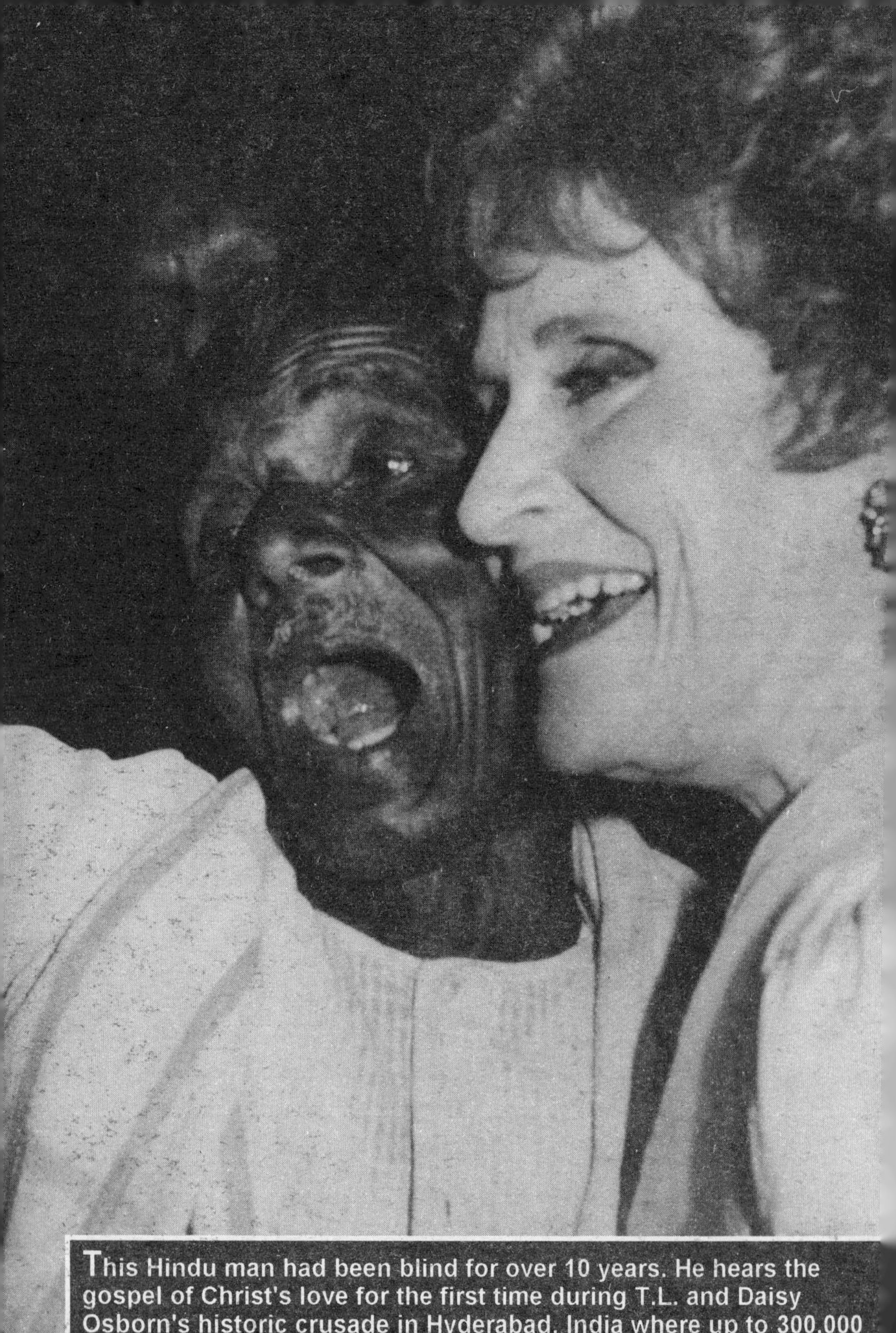

This Hindu man had been blind for over 10 years. He hears the gospel of Christ's love for the first time during T.L. and Daisy Osborn's historic crusade in Hyderabad, India where up to 300,000 people attend each great public meeting. He embraces Jesus as his Savior and Lord, and his sight is now miraculously restored. Daisy rejoices with him as he witnesses to the multitude present.

He was born both deaf and mute. In the Osborns' Hyderabad Crusade, he watched people being healed in each meeting. He followed the Osborns to their car each night. In sign language they encouraged him. Now he has been miraculously healed. He yells as loudly as he can, thrilled to hear his own voice. In great emotion and tears of joy, he embraces T.L. to thank him for his miracle.

T.L. AND DAISY OSBORN *MASS-MIRACLE CRUSADES* WORLDWIDE
The Osborns *Mass Crusades* have brought new faith, hope and love to millions of people in over 70 nations. They consistently go out in public parks, stadiums and open fields to proclaim the gospel, where all peoples of all faiths may attend and see, for themselves, the gospel confirmed by signs and miracles, wrought by Christ's power today.

S. PACIFIC — Surabaya, Indonesia

EUROPE — The Hague, Holland

AFRICA — Uyo, Nigeria

S. AMERICA — Bogota, Colombia

ASIA — Hyderabad, India

T.L. and Daisy Osborn Crusade, Kampala, Uganda.

"And a great multitude followed him, because they saw his miracles which he did on them that were diseased." John 6:2

"Many believed in his name, when they saw the miracles which he did." John 2:23

"And by the hands of the apostles were many signs and wonders wrought among the people; ... And believers were the more added to the Lord, multitudes both of men and women." Acts 5:12,14

Dr. T.L. Osborn and Dr. Daisy Osborn, "teaching and preaching the gospel of the kingdom" at the Lugogo Stadium in Kampala.

Daisy teaches thousands of African women during her National Women's Ministry Seminar in Kenya's Nyanza province.

Daisy Osborn conducts a National Women's mass meeting at Kampala, with over 200,000 women in attendance—besides men and children.

Daisy conducts a National Women's Conference at Accra, Ghana.

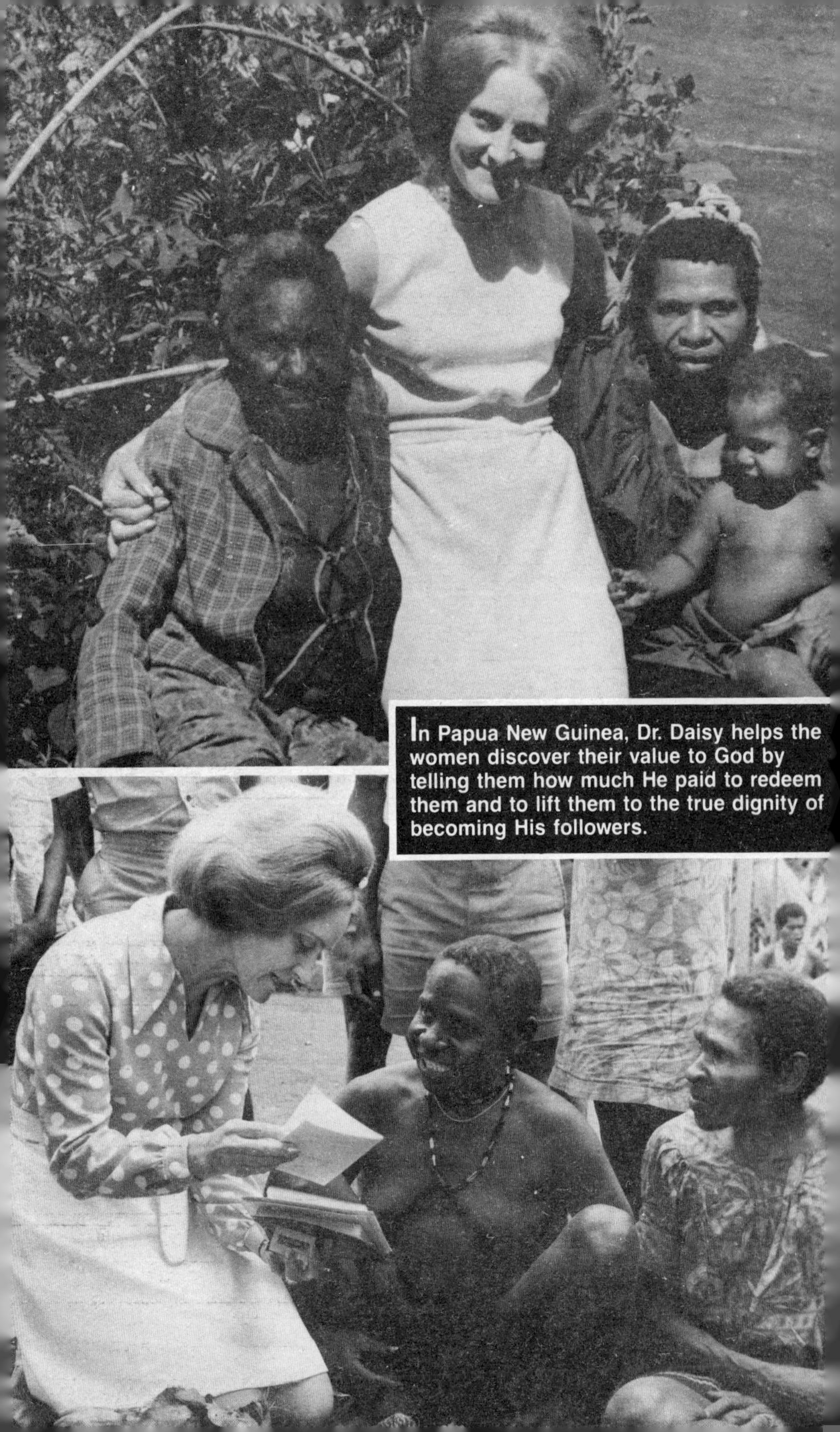

In Papua New Guinea, Dr. Daisy helps the women discover their value to God by telling them how much He paid to redeem them and to lift them to the true dignity of becoming His followers.

"God never left Himself without a witness; there were always His reminders." Ac.14:17 Living Bible

"He sent us to preach the Good News everywhere and to testify that ... everyone who believes in Him will have their sins forgiven through His name." Ac.10 42-43 Living Bible

T.L. AND DAISY OSBORN EVANGELISM CRUSADES WORLDWIDE.
In 73 different nations of the world, great multitudes always throng their meetings to hear God's word and to be blessed by Him.

Djakarta, Java, Indonesia
Yaba, Lagos, Nigeria, W. Africa
Hyderabad, Andhra Pradesh, India
Tainan, Taiwan
Guatemala City, Guatemala, Central America

God created man and woman for excellence, success, exhilaration, self-esteem, health, happiness and abundance in His *Good Life*. He never designed His own offspring, made *"in his own likeness and image,"* for mediocrity, insignificance, disease, poverty or guilt.

From the breathtaking grandeur of mountain peaks to the fabulous rich valleys of our planet, God placed humanity amidst a rich world of GOOD things for their usefulness, beauty and pleasure.

He said: *"Instead of shame and dishonor, you shall have a double portion of prosperity and everlasting joy, and all shall realize that you are a people God has blessed."* Isa.61:7,9 Living Bible

"If you want a happy, GOOD LIFE, ... trust yourself to Christ your Lord." 1Pet.3:10,15 Living Bible

"No GOOD thing will He withhold from them that walk uprightly before Him." Psalm 84:11

PART

V

HEALTH FOR GOD'S SERVICE

THE GOOD LIFE that God created you for, includes robust physical health for His glory.

Thousands of people succumb to sickness and suffering without ever questioning its source.

A good God simply cannot show favoritism anymore than a good parent can. Blessings provided by the death of Christ must be equally available to every person for whom Christ died.

God's promises express His will for us.

➡

Chapter 16

The Man Who Rose from the Dead

THE GOOD LIFE really began the day Jesus Christ was raised from the dead according to the scriptures.

Some of the most exciting days in Jerusalem's history followed the resurrection of Christ from the dead.

Rumors were running wild that this man Jesus, who had been executed as a criminal had risen from the dead.

Every day, matters were getting worse.

First, it was the tale of the woman who said she saw Him alive.[Mt.28:5-8]

Then the disciples claimed they had touched Him and had witnessed Him eat meat.[Lu.24:36-43]

At Pentecost, the disciples had just received the baptism of the Holy Ghost.[Ac.2:1-4]

An emotional crowd had witnessed these simple Galileans speaking in the tongues of all the nations of the known world.[Ac.2:5-12]

The captain of the soldiers became nervous as he pondered the constant stream of reports coming into his office.

"I saw that man crucified, myself," he muttered as he filed another report. "I saw Him bleed. I know the man who made the final check and thrust the spear in His side. He is dead. He is bound to be dead." *Jn.19:31-36*

The door opened and another soldier rushed in.

"Sir, I hate to admit it but I'm afraid there is something to this," he begins.

The captain barks his interruption: "Something to what? Speak up."

"Jesus," he continues, "must be alive again. I know, sir, it sounds foolish, but there are so many things happening these days. I don't know, maybe I'd better take a leave of absence."

"Leave of absence?" the captain blurts. "This thing is getting out of hand fast. I may need every soldier in town on duty before nightfall. The high priests and the Sanhedrin are in session today trying to decide on their position in the face of this confusion.

"Don't you know that if it's proven that Jesus is alive again, the whole country will follow Him? Don't you realize that it would prove all that He claimed? Do you understand the religious war we would be faced with?" *Mt.28:11-15*

Just then a messenger arrived with a complaint that a large crowd was gathering down at Solomon's Porch and that an attempt to disperse them had failed.[Ac.3:11]

"What caused it?" demanded the captain.

"It's those two men who caused that big commotion the other day during the celebration of Pentecost, when so many heard them speak languages, and saw fire on their heads," the messenger replied.[Ac.2:1-12]

"Well, what are they up to this time?" the captain inquired further.

"Sir, it's that crippled beggar from the temple gate ...," he hesitated.[Ac.3:1-9]

"They didn't heal him, did they?" the captain asked.

"Yes, sir," the messenger stated, "I saw him get up and walk around, run and jump. He was ... well, it was just like it was in the market when Jesus was healing the people." [Ac.3:8]

"Jesus, Jesus," the captain slowly shook his head, "every time I turn around I hear something about Jesus."

"Those two men, Peter and John," he asked, "did they make any statements?"

"Well, sir, the one called Peter was trying to explain that he didn't perform the cure; that it was by the power of Jesus." Ac.3:12-16

The captain broke in again. "What did he say about Jesus?"

The leader called Peter explained, *People of Israel, why do you marvel at this? or why do you look so earnestly on us as though by our own power or holiness we had made this man to walk? The God of Abraham, and of Isaac, and of Jacob, the God of our fathers, has glorified his Son Jesus; you denied the Holy One and killed the Prince of life, whom God has raised from the dead; whereof we are witnesses. And his name, through faith in his name has made this man strong, whom you see and know; yes, the faith which is by Jesus has given him this perfect soundness in the presence of you all. Repent therefore, and be converted, that your sins may be blotted out.* Ac.3:12-17,19

The captain looked up. A worried look was on his face. He had to disperse that mob at any cost. His duty required it.

Rumors were everywhere. "He is risen." "He is alive." "He still has power." "He is with His disciples." "He is healing again."

None of the soldiers had seen Jesus. But they were all becoming skittish. They were afraid they might see Him. It would be like a murderer meeting a victim.

The captain decided to take action and he ordered that meeting be ended.

The priests, the captain of the temple, and the Sadducees came upon them, being grieved that they taught the people, and preached through Jesus the resurrection from the dead. And they laid hands on them, and put them in hold to the next day: for it was now evening.

However, many of them which heard the word believed; and the number was about five thousand.[Ac.4:1-4]

The next day in court, the high priest asked Peter: *By what power, or by what name, have you done this?* [Ac.4:7]

Peter answered firmly: *Be it known to you all, that by the name of Jesus Christ of Nazareth, whom you crucified, whom God raised from the dead, even by him does this man stand here before you whole.*[Ac.4:10]

Noting Peter and John's boldness, yet knowing they were uneducated non-professionals, the court marveled *and took knowledge of them, that they had been with Jesus. And beholding the man which was healed standing with them, they could say nothing against it.*[Ac.4:13-14]

With great power the apostles gave witness (proof) *of the resurrection of the Lord Jesus.*[Ac.4:33]

You see, in those days, only one thing mattered: Prove that Jesus had risen. The resurrection was not taken for granted.

To the contrary, it was bitterly opposed and flatly denied.

By the hands of the apostles were many signs and

wonders wrought among the people (and believers were added to the Lord, multitudes both of men and women). Insomuch that they brought forth the sick into the streets, and laid them on beds and couches, that at the least the shadow of Peter passing by might overshadow some of them. There came also a multitude out of the cities round about to Jerusalem, bringing sick folks, and them which were vexed with unclean spirits: and they were healed every one.[Ac.5:12-16]

Every time another miracle was witnessed, the disciples declared that it was further proof that Jesus had risen according to the scriptures.

Jesus was risen, but the people had to have the evidence before they would believe. There was one proof then; there is one proof today — miracles in His name.

If He is dead, He can do no miracles. If He is alive, then He will do the same things today that He did before He was crucified.

Multitudes were convinced, and turned to the Lord.[Ac.2:41; Ac.8:6-8; Ac.9:42; Ac.11:21; Ac.13:48; Ac.16:34; Ac.17:12; Ac.18:8; Ac.19:18-20]

Thus, Christianity was born and multiplied.

The message was heralded by those who knew that they could not make disciples of a dead Christ; that if people were to believe on Christ, they must be convinced that He is risen and alive.

The only way to convince them was for Him to

do the same works that He did before He died.[Ac.3:6, 14-16]

And so the early church was born in miracles.

If the millions of our generation are to believe on Christ, they must witness the proof that *Jesus Christ is the same yesterday and to day and forever.*[He.13:8]

Christ lives today. He has never changed. Do you believe this?[Jn.11:26]

If you can believe, all things are possible to those that believe.[Mk.9:23]

For if there is no resurrection of the dead, then Christ must still be dead.

And if he is still dead, then all our preaching is useless and your trust in God is empty, worthless, hopeless; and we apostles are all liars because we have said that God raised Christ from the grave, and of course that isn't true if the dead do not come back to life again.

If they don't, then Christ is still dead, and you are very foolish to keep on trusting God to save you, and you are still under condemnation for your sins; in that case all Christians who have died are lost.

And if being a Christian is of value to us only now in this life, we are the most miserable of creatures.

But the fact is that Christ did actually rise from the dead, and has become the first of millions who will come back to life again some day.[1Co.15:13-20 LB]

For if you tell others with your own mouth that Jesus Christ is your Lord, and believe in your own heart that God has raised him from the dead, you will be saved.

For it is by believing in your heart that you become right with God; and with your mouth you tell others of your faith, confirming your salvation.

For the scriptures tell us that no one who believes in Christ will ever be disappointed. Jew and Gentile are the same in this respect: they all have the same Lord who generously gives his riches to all those who ask him for them. Anyone who calls on the name of the Lord will be saved.[Ro.10:9-13 LB]

Chapter 17

Healing for Everyone

THE GOOD LIFE includes physical health.

It is God's will for the new Christian to be physically healed as well as to be spiritually saved.

Who forgives all your iniquities; who heals all your diseases.[Ps.103:3]

Healing and forgiveness are gifts of God which are to be received by faith.

Faith is expecting God to do what He promised to do. That is why *faith comes by hearing the word of God.*[Ro.10:17]

God has given to us His great and abundant promises [2Pe.1:4] in order to reveal to us His will. His testament or His will or His promise or His word is all the same.

In order to receive any blessing of the good life from God, it must come to us by faith. To have faith for any blessing, we must be convinced that such a blessing is God's will for us. As long as we have a question about whether or not God wills that we receive something, we cannot have faith.

We are commanded to ask for things, believing that we receive them. *Ask in faith, nothing wavering. For if you waver, you are like a wave of the sea driven of the wind and tossed. So let not such a person think they shall receive anything of the Lord.*[Ja.1:6-7]

You cannot be saved until you believe that God loves you and that Christ died for your sins; until you are sure that it is, therefore, God's will and desire to forgive you. You then accept this gift of new life by faith and you are born again. You know salvation is for *whoever will.*[Jn.3:16; Ro.10:13; Re.22:17] It is for everyone.

In the same way, if you are sick, you must be convinced by the promises of God that it is His will to heal you physically. Otherwise you will not be able to ask in faith.

Religious tradition teaches that you should ask for healing by praying, "if it be God's will." Consequently, very few people experience healing miracles.

But God has abundantly promised physical healing for His children.

Clearly, according to the Bible, the good life includes physical health for God's glory.

Notice what happened shortly after Christ was raised from the dead. It is an example of what God's will is wherever the gospel is preached.

And by the hands of the apostles were many signs

and wonders done among the people.

And believers were added to the Lord, multitudes both of men and women:

Insomuch that they brought forth the sick into the streets, and laid them on beds and couches, that at the least the shadow of Peter passing by might overshadow some of them.

There came also a multitude out of the cities round about to Jerusalem, bringing sick folks, and them which were vexed with unclean spirits: and they were healed everyone.[Ac.5:12-16]

These words, *they were healed everyone,* reveal what God's will is today for all who are sick.

This is a record of what was accomplished under Peter's ministry in Jerusalem after Jesus had returned to the Father. *They were healed everyone.*

It was a testimony that Christ's ministry had not changed after His ascension.

They were healed everyone was a fulfillment of God's healing covenant: *I am the Lord that heals you.*[Ex.15:26] *You* in that covenant included *everyone* in Jerusalem under Peter's ministry.

They were healed everyone was experienced by the entire nation of Israel: *There was not one feeble person among their tribes.*[Ps.105:37]

It was experienced by everyone in the throngs which followed Jesus: *Great multitudes followed him and he healed them all.*[Mt.12:15]

This is what happened to *everyone* of the Israelites who were bit by the fiery serpents: *When they beheld the serpent of brass lifted up on a pole,* (a type of Calvary)[Jn.3:14-15] *they lived.*[Nu.21:8-9]

This is what happened when *He sent his word and healed them.*[Ps.107:20] That is the purpose of His word concerning healing being sent to you today; so that *everyone* will be healed.

They were healed everyone is the promise for today. It includes you. It will save you from a premature death: *I will take sickness away from the midst of you, the number of your days I will fulfill.*[Ex.23:25-26]

To make it possible for *everyone* to be healed, *Christ has redeemed us from the curse of the law.*[Ga.3:13] This curse included *every sickness and every plague.*[De.28:61] *Us* includes *everyone.*

This blessing was provided for *everyone* at Calvary when *certainly he suffered our pains and carried our diseases.*[Is.53:4 LT]

This was made possible because *with his stripes we are healed.*[Is.53:5; 1Pe.2:24] *We* includes *everyone.*

This was made possible when *Himself took our infirmities; and bore our sicknesses.*[Mt.8:17] *Our* includes *everyone.*

When Christ *came down from heaven, not to do* (His) *own will, but the will of him that sent* (Him);

[Jn.6:38] He repeatedly *healed them all.*[Mt.12:15; Mt.14:36; Lu.6:19; Ac.10:38] His own ministry on earth established His will to heal *everyone.*

They were healed everyone was the standard in Christ's ministry. It was what He promised to the believing church. *They that believe on me, the works that I do shall they do also.*[Jn.14:12]

They were healed everyone was what *Jesus began both to do and teach, until the day in which he was taken up,*[Ac.1:1-2] and then continued to do after He was taken up and seated at the Father's right hand.[Ac.5:16; Ac.28:9]

They were healed everyone is therefore the will of God now while Christ is seated in heaven: *Jesus Christ the same yesterday, and to day, and for ever.*[He.13:8]

They were healed everyone is as much the will of God as it is His will to forgive every sinner who repents. *Who forgives all, who heals all.*[Ps.103:3]

They were healed everyone. This blessing is for every city: *In whatever city you enter, heal the sick that are there.*[Lu.10:8-9] *The sick* includes *everyone* who is sick.

They were healed everyone. This puts whole cities to talking about Jesus, and makes Him the center of attraction by the public, as was the case in Jerusalem.

They were healed everyone will bring *multitudes* to

hear the gospel.[Ac.5:16] It will also bring multitudes from surrounding towns and cities.

They were healed everyone. In this way *multitudes both of men and women* are *added to the Lord.*[Ac.5:14] The first healing miracle in Acts caused *about five thousand* people to *believe.*[Ac.4:4]

They were healed everyone is one of the ways by which God bore witness to this great salvation *both with signs and wonders, and with divers miracles, and gifts of the Holy Ghost.*[He.2:3-4]

This is the ministry which has caused multiplied thousands of non-Christians to obey the gospel in our own crusades in 73 countries of the world.

They were healed everyone. The early church prayed for this before the sick were brought from the surrounding areas to the streets of Jerusalem for healing. *By stretching forth your hand to heal; and that signs and wonders may be done by the name of your holy child Jesus.*[Ac.4:29-30]

They were healed everyone. Even the physically well and strong united to bring about this result. *They brought the sick to the streets, and laid them on beds and couches.*[Ac.5:15]

They were healed everyone. This is what the whole church is to pray for *in one accord,* as the early church did: *They lifted up their voice to God with one accord.*[Ac.4:24]

They were healed everyone. This was accomplished for all when the sick did not get as close to Peter as the people got to Jesus, when *they laid the sick in the streets, and sought him that they might touch but the border of his garment; and as many as touched him were made whole.*[Mk.6:56] They did not even touch Peter, only *the shadow of Peter,* yet *they were healed everyone* and there were *multitudes* of them.

They were healed everyone. This is the result the Holy Spirit longs to accomplish everywhere: a) He interceded for it; [Ac.4:24-30] b) He accomplished it; [Ac.5:12-16] and, c) He recorded it so that every creature could hear and read about it, and thus have faith for it to be repeated today.

They were healed everyone would have included you, if you were sick, and if you had been there that day. Healing, therefore, is for you today, because God's will which was executed in Jerusalem has never changed.

They were healed everyone included all of *them which were vexed with unclean spirits.*[Ac.5:16] The demon possessed are included in God's will for healing today.

They were healed everyone. These words could not be used in recording Jesus' ministry at Nazareth: *He could do no mighty work there except that he laid his hands on a few sick people, and healed them. And he marveled because of their unbelief.*[Mk.6:5-6; Mt.13:58]

Only a *few sick people* were healed in Nazareth. Where the individual's attitude was wrong, the result under Jesus' ministry was not as good as under Peter's ministry when the individual's attitude was right.

They were healed everyone. This result can be the same today when *everyone* believes the truth about healing. Jesus said: *You shall know the truth and the truth shall make you free.*[Jn.8:32]

They were healed everyone. This is included in Christ's promise: *Those who come to me, I will not cast out.*[Jn.6:37] Every sick person in Jerusalem and from the cities round about Jerusalem,[Ac.5:15-16] and in the villages, cities and country[Mk.6:56] proved that this blessing was for them.

They were healed everyone. To extend this blessing to you, Christ commands you: *Have faith in God.*[Mk.11:22] His words to you are: *According to your faith be it done to you.*[Mt.9:29] He promises, *when you pray, believe that you receive* (what you ask for), *and you shall have them.*[Mk.11:24] He says, *Ask what you will, and it shall be done to you.*[Jn.15:7]

They were healed everyone. This is God's will today. It is His will for you now. He promises, *everyone that asks receives.*[Mt.7:8]

Chapter 18

Healing for Today

TO ENJOY THE FULLNESS of God's goodness and receive the physical healing God wills for you to have, one of the most important steps is to know that the age of miracles has not passed, and that physical healing is part of Christ's ministry today.

In Bible days, the sick were healed, blind received their sight, deaf were made to hear, cripples walked, lepers were cleansed, and all manner of sick and suffering people were made whole by God's power. These miracles are as much for the church today as they ever were.

There are five basic reasons why we can know this:

1. God is a healer,[Ex.15:26] and He has never changed: *I am the Lord, I change not.*[Mal.3:6]

2. Jesus Christ healed the sick,[Mt.9:35; Mk.6:55-56; Ac.10:38] and He has never changed: *Jesus Christ the same yesterday, and to day, and for ever.*[He.13:8]

3. Jesus commanded His disciples to heal the sick,[Mt.10:1-7; Lu.10:1, 9] and a true disciple of Christ is

the same today as then: *If you continue in my word, then you are my disciples indeed.*[Jn.8:31]

4. Miracles of healing were manifested everywhere in the ministry of the early church,[Ac.3:6; Ac.4:30; Ac.5:12; Ac.6:8; Ac.8:6; Ac.14:3, 9-10; Ac.19:11-12; He.2:4] and the true church has never changed. The life and ministry of the apostles is the example and pattern for the true church *to the end of the world.*[Mt.28:20]

5. Jesus commissioned all believers, among all nations, to the end of the world, to lay their hands on the sick, promising *they shall recover,*[Mk.16:15-18] and certainly true believers have never changed. Jesus said, *Those that believe on me, the works that I do shall they do also.*[Jn.14:12]

Divine healing was administered first by Jehovah-God, then by His Son, Jesus Christ, next by His disciples, later by the early church, and last by all believers in all the world. Therefore, the age of miracles has not passed and physical healing is as much a part of Christ's ministry today as it ever was. What He has done for so many tens of thousands of others, it is His will to do for you.

Chapter 19

100 Facts About Healing

MANY BELIEVE THAT God sometimes heals the sick, but they have no personal knowledge of Jesus as the indwelling ever-present healer. They know nothing about the many facts which prove that physical healing is part of everyone's salvation.

They see others healed, but they question whether healing is God's will for them. They are waiting for a special revelation of the will of God concerning their case, and in the meantime they are doing all within the power of human skill to get well, with the use of natural means, whether they think it is God's will for them to be healed or not.

If it is not God's will for them to be well, why do they seek recovery through medical science?

If healing is God's will, then all healing is from God whether one recovers health through the aid of medical science, or by prayer and faith in God's promises.

The Bible reveals the will of God in regard to the healing of the body as clearly as it reveals the will of God in regard to the saving of the soul. God need not give a special revelation of His will when He has plainly promised it in His word. His promises to heal are as much a revelation of His will to heal as His promises to save reveal His will to save.

A careful study of the scriptures will clearly show that God is both the savior and the healer of His people; that it is always His will to save and to heal all those who are willing to serve Him. In evidence of this, we call your attention to the following 100 facts:

1. Sickness is no more natural than sin. God made all things *very good.*[Ge.1:31] Therefore, we should not conclude that the only remedy for sin or sickness is in the natural, but that God who created us happy, strong, healthy and in fellowship with himself, is the healer of our physical diseases as much as He is the Savior for our spiritual sins.

2. Both sin and sickness came into the world through the fall of the human race. Therefore, we must look for the healing of both in the Savior.

3. When God called His children out of Egypt, He made a covenant of healing with them.[Ex.15:26; Ex.23:25] All through their history, we find them in sickness and in pestilence turning to God in repentance and confession and always, when their sins were forgiven, their sicknesses were healed.

4. God healed those who were bitten by fiery serpents, through a look at a brazen serpent on a pole, which was a type of Calvary.[Nu.21:8; Jn.3:14-15] If everyone who looked at the brazen serpent was healed then, it is logical that everyone who looks to Jesus can be healed today.

5. Jesus said: *As Moses lifted up the serpent in the wilderness, even so* (for the same purpose) *must the Son of man be lifted up.*[Jn.3:14; Nu.21:4-9]

6. The people had sinned against God then; people have sinned against God today.

7. The poison serpent's bite resulted in death then; *the wages of sin is death* today.[Ro.6:23]

8. The people cried to God then, and He heard their cry and provided a remedy, the serpent lifted up; those who cry to God today discover that God has heard their cry and has provided them a remedy, Christ lifted up.

9. The remedy was for *everyone that is bitten* then. The remedy is for *whoever believes* today.

10. In their remedy they received both forgiveness for their sins, and healing for their bodies; in Christ, we receive both forgiveness for our sins, and healing for our sick bodies today.

11. There were no exceptions then. Their remedy was for *everyone that is bitten*. There are no exceptions today. Our remedy is for *whoever believes*.

12. Everyone was commanded to do their own looking at the remedy then. Everyone is commanded to do their own believing on Christ to-

day.

13. They did not need to beg, nor make an offering to God then. There was only one condition — *when you look.* We do not need to beg nor make an offering to Christ today. There is only one condition — *whoever believes.*

14. They were not told to look to Moses, but rather to the remedy then. We are not told to look to the preacher or priest, but to Christ today.

15. They were not to look to the symptoms of their snake bites then, but rather, to their remedy. We are not to look to the symptoms of our sin and disease today, but to our remedy, Christ.

16. *Everyone that is bitten, when they look on it, shall live,* was the promise to all then, without exception. *Whoever believes on him shall not perish, but have everlasting life* [Jn.3:16] is the promise to all today, without exception.

17. Since their curse was removed by the lifting up of the "type" of Calvary, our curse was certainly removed by Calvary itself.[Ga.3:13]

18. The "type" of Calvary could not mean more to those Israelites then, than Calvary means to us today. Surely they could not receive blessings through only a "type" of Calvary which we cannot receive through Calvary itself.

19. God promises protection for our bodies as well as our souls, if we abide in Him.[Ps.91] In the

New Testament John wishes *above all things that you may prosper and be in health, even as your soul prospers.*[3Jn.2] Both scriptures show that God's will is that we be as healthy in our bodies as we are in our souls. It is never God's will for our souls to be sick; it is never God's will for our bodies to be sick.

20. Asa died in his sickness, because he sought *not to the Lord, but to the physicians,*[2Chr.16:12] while Hezekiah lived, *because he sought not to the physicians, but to the Lord.*[Is.38:1-5]

21. The removal of our diseases is included in Christ's atonement, along with the removal of our sins.[Is.53:4-5] The word *bore* implies substitution, suffering for; not sympathy, suffering with. If Christ bore our sicknesses, why should we bear them?

22. Christ fulfilled Isaiah's words, *healing all that were sick.*[Mt.8:16-17]

23. Sickness is revealed as coming directly from Satan: *Satan went forth and smote Job with sore boils from the sole of his foot to his crown.*[Jb.2:7] Job maintained steadfast faith as he cried out to God for deliverance, and he was healed.[Jb.42:10,12]

24. Christ declared that the infirm woman was bound by Satan and ought to be loosed. He cast out the *spirit of the infirmity* and she was healed.[Lu.13:11-13, 16]

25. A devil which possessed a man was the cause of him being both blind and dumb. When the devil was cast out, he could both see and talk.[Mt.12:22]

26. A demon was the cause of a boy being deaf and dumb and also the cause of his convulsions. When the demon was cast out, the boy was healed.[Mk.9:17-26]

27. The Bible says, *Jesus of Nazareth went about healing all that were oppressed of the devil.*[Ac.10:38] This scripture shows that sickness is Satan's oppression.

28. We are told that *the Son of God was manifested, that he might destroy the works of the devil.*[1Jn.3:8] Sickness is part of Satan's *works.* Christ, in His earthly ministry, always treated sin, disease and devils the same; they were all hateful in His sight; He rebuked them all; He was manifested to destroy them all.

29. He does not want the *works of the devil* to continue in our physical bodies today, since He came and was manifested to destroy these works. He does not want a cancer, a plague, a curse, *the works of the devil,* to exist in His own members. *Don't you know that your bodies are the members of Christ?*[1Co.6:15]

30. Jesus said, *The Son of man is not come to destroy lives, but to save them.*[Lu.9:56] Sickness destroys, therefore it is not from God. Christ came to *save*

us. The Greek word, sozo, means to deliver us, to save and preserve us, to heal us, to give us life, to make us whole; but never to *destroy* us.

31. Jesus said, *The thief* (speaking of Satan) *comes not, but for to steal, and to kill, and to destroy: I am come that they might have life, and that they might have it more abundantly.*[Jn.10:10]

32. Satan is a killer; his diseases are the destroyers of life; his sicknesses are the thieves of happiness, health, money, time and effort. Christ came to give us abundant life in our souls, and in our bodies.

33. We are promised the *life of Jesus* in *our mortal flesh.*[2Co.4:10-11]

34. We are taught that the Spirit's work is to quicken our mortal bodies in this life.[Ro.8:11]

35. Satan's work is to kill; Christ's work is to give life.

36. Satan is bad. God is good. Bad things come from Satan. Good things come from God.

37. Sickness is, therefore, from Satan. Health is, therefore, from God.

38. All authority and power over all demons and disease has been given to every disciple of Christ.[Mt.10:1; Mk.16:17; Lu.10:19] Since Jesus said, *If you continue in my word, then are you my disciples indeed,*[Jn.8:31] therefore, these scriptures apply to you today, that is, if you continue in (act on) His

word.

39. The right to pray and receive the answer is given to every believer: *If you shall ask anything in my name, I will do it.*[Jn.14:13-14] This logically includes asking for healing, if one is sick.

40. *Everyone that asks receives.*[Mt.7:8] That promise is for you. It includes everyone who is sick.

41. The ministry of healing was given to the seventy, who represent the future workers of the church.[Lu.10:1,9, 19]

42. It was given to all *them that believe* the gospel; *them that act* on the gospel, or the *practicers* or *doers* of the word.[Mk.16:17; Lu.6:47-48; Ro.2:13; Ja.1:22-24]

43. It is committed to the elders of the church.[Ja.5:14]

44. It is bestowed upon the whole church as one of its ministries and gifts, until Jesus comes.[1Co.12:9-10]

45. Jesus never commissioned anyone to preach the gospel without commanding that they heal the sick. He said: *Into whatever city you enter, heal the sick that are there.*[Lu.10:8-9] That command applies to the true ministry today.

46. Jesus said that He would continue His same works through believers while He is with the Father; *Verily, verily, I say to you, they that believe on me, the works that I do shall they do also; and greater works than these shall they do; because I go to*

my Father.[Jn.14:12] This certainly includes healing the sick.

47. In connection with the Lord's Supper, the cup is taken *in remembrance* of His blood which was shed for the remission of our sins.[1Co.11:25] The bread is eaten *in remembrance* of His body on which were laid our diseases and the stripes by which *we are healed.*[1Co.11:23-24; Is.53:5]

48. Jesus said that certain teachers *make the word of God of none effect through* (their) *traditions.*[Mk.7:13] For centuries human ideas and theories have hindered the healing portion of the gospel from being proclaimed and acted on as it was by the early church.

49. One tradition is that God wills some of His children to suffer sickness and that, therefore, many who are prayed for are not healed because it is not His will to heal them. When Jesus healed the demon-possessed boy in Mark, chapter nine, whom the disciples could not heal,[Mk.9:18] He proved that it is God's will to heal even those who fail to receive healing. Furthermore, He assigned the failure of the disciples to cure the boy, not to God's will, but to the disciples' *unbelief.*[Mt.17:19-20]

50. The failure of many to be healed today when prayed for is never because it is not God's will to heal them.

51. If sickness is the will of God, then every

physician would be a lawbreaker, every trained nurse a defier of the Almighty and every hospital a house of rebellion instead of a house of mercy.

52. Since Christ came to do the Father's will,[Jn.6:38; He.10:7, 9] the fact that He *healed them all* is proof that it is God's will that all be healed.

53. If it is not God's will for all to be healed, how did *everyone* in the *multitudes* obtain from Christ what it was not God's will for some of them to receive? The gospel says, *He healed them all.*

54. If it is not God's will for all to be healed, why do the scriptures state: *With his stripes we are healed* [Is.53:5] and *by whose stripes you were healed?* [1Pe.2:24] How could *we* and *you* be declared healed, if it is God's will for some of us to be sick?

55. Christ never refused those who sought His healing. Repeatedly the Gospels tell us that *He healed them all.*[Mt.8:16; Mt.9:35; Mt.12:15; Mk.6:55-56; Lu.4:40; Ac.10:38] Christ the healer has never changed.[He.13:8]

56. Only one person in the entire Bible ever asked for healing saying, *If it be your will. That was the leper to whom Jesus immediately responded, I will; be clean.*[Mk.1:40-41]

57. Another tradition is that we can glorify God more by being patient in our sickness than by being healed. If sickness glorifies God more than healing, then any attempt to get well by natural

or divine means would be an effort to rob God of the glory that we should want Him to receive.

58. If sickness glorifies God, then we should rather be sick than well.

59. If sickness glorifies God, Jesus robbed His Father of all the glory that He could by healing everyone,[Lu.4:40] and the Holy Spirit continued doing the same throughout the Acts of the Apostles.[Ac.5:12-16]

60. Paul says, *You are bought with a price; therefore glorify God in your body, and in your spirit, which are God's.*[1Co.6:20]

61. Both our body and our spirit are bought with a price. We are to glorify God in both.

62. We do not glorify God in our *spirit* by remaining in sin; neither do we glorify God in our *body* by remaining sick.

63. The sickness and death of Lazarus is used by some to prove that sickness glorifies God. But God was not glorified in this case until Lazarus was raised up from the dead, the result of which *many* of the Jews *believed on Jesus.*[Jn.11:4, 45]

64. Another tradition is that while God heals some, it is not His will to heal all. But Jesus, who came to do the Father's will, did *heal them all.*[Jn.6:38; Mt.8:16; Mt.12:15; Lu.4:40; Lu.6:19]

65. If healing is not for all, why did Jesus bear our sicknesses, our pains, and our diseases? [Is.53:4;

[Mt.8:17] If God wanted some of His children to suffer, then Jesus relieved us from bearing something which God wanted us to bear. But since Jesus came to do the *will of the Father,* and since He *has borne our diseases,* it must be God's will for all to be well.

66. If it is not God's will for all to be healed, then God's promises to heal are not for all; that would mean that *faith* (does not come) *by hearing the word of God* (alone), but by getting a special revelation that God has favored you and wills to heal you.

67. If God's promises to heal are not for all, that means that we cannot know what God's will is by reading His word alone; that we must pray until He speaks directly to us about each case in particular. That means we must close our Bibles and pray for a direct revelation from God to know if it is His will to heal each case. That would virtually mean we could not consider God's word as directed to us personally. Would that be right? Never, because God's word is for all.

68. God's word is His will. God's promises reveal His will. When we read of what He promises to do, then we know what it is His will to do.

69. Since it is written: *Faith comes by hearing the word of God,*[Ro.10:17] then the best way to build faith in your heart that God is willing to heal you is for you to hear that part of God's word which prom-

ises healing.

70. Faith for spiritual healing *comes by hearing* the gospel – He *bore our sins.*[1Pe.2:24] Faith for physical healing *comes by hearing* the gospel – He *bore our sicknesses.*[Mt.8:17]

71. Therefore, we are to *preach the gospel* (that He bore our sins) *to every creature.*[Mk.16:15] We are to *preach the gospel* (that He bore our sicknessess) *to every creature.*[Mk.16:15]

72. Christ emphasized His promise, *If you shall ask anything in my name, I will do it,* by repeating it twice.[Jn.14:13-14] He did not exclude healing from this promise. *Anything* includes healing. This promise is for all.

73. If healing is not for all, Christ should have qualified His promise accordingly, and said, *Whatever things you desire* (except healing), *when you pray, believe that you receive them, and you shall have them.*[Mk.11:24] But He did not. Healing, therefore, is included in the *whatever.* This promise is made to you.

74. If it is not God's will to heal all, Christ's promise would not be dependable where He said, *If you live in me, and my words live in you, ask what you will, and it shall be done to you.*[Jn.15:7]

75. The Bible says: *Is any sick among you? Call for the elders of the church; and let them pray, anointing the sick with oil in the name of the Lord: and the*

prayer of faith shall save the sick, and the Lord shall raise them up.[Ja.5:14-15] This promise is for all, including you, if you are sick.

76. If God today has abandoned healing in answer to prayer in favor of healing only by medical science, that would mean that He requires us to use a less successful method during a better dispensation. The Bible says that we now have a *better hope,*[He.7:19] a *better testament,*[He.7:22] a *better covenant which is established upon better promises.*[He.8:6] He healed them all then, but today many diseases are incurable by medical science.

77. Paul tells us that God would have us *perfect in every good work,*[He.13:21] and *abounding to every good work.*[2Co.9:8] A sick person cannot measure up to these scriptures. These conditions would be impossible if healing is not for all. Either healing is not for all, or these scriptures do not apply to all.

78. Bodily healing in the New Testament was called a *mercy,* and it was His mercy which always moved Him to heal all the sick. His promise is, *He is plenteous in mercy to all that call on Him.*[Ps.86:5] That includes you, today.

79. The literal translation of Isaiah, chapter fifty-three, verse four is: *Surely* (or certainly) *he has borne our sicknesses, and carried our pains.* To prove that our sicknesses were carried away, the same Hebrew verb for *bore* and *carried* is used to de-

scribe both. (See verses 11-12.)

80. Christ was *made sin for us* [2Co.5:21] when *He bore our sins.* [1Pe.2:24] He was *made a curse for us* [Ga.3:13] when *He bore our sicknesses.* [Mt.8:17]

81. Since Christ *bore our sins,* how many is it God's will to forgive? *Whoever believes.* Since Christ *bore our sicknesses,* how many is it God's will to heal? *He heals them all.*

82. Another tradition is that if we are righteous, we should accept sickness as a part of our life. They quote the scripture: *Many are the afflictions of the righteous.* [Ps.34:19] But this does not mean sicknesses as some would have us believe. It means trials, hardships, persecutions, temptations, but never sickness or physical disability.

83. It would be a contradiction to say that Christ has borne our sicknesses, and with His stripes we are healed, and then to add, *Many are the* (sicknesses) *of the righteous,* which He requires us to bear.

84. To prove this tradition, a verse sometimes quoted is: *But the God of all grace, who has called us to his eternal glory by Christ Jesus, after that you have suffered a while, make you perfect, establish, strengthen and settle you.* [1Pe.5:10] This suffering does not refer to suffering sickness, but to the many ways in which God's people have so often had to suffer for their testimony. [Ac.5:41; Ac.7:57-60; Ac.8:1; 2Co.11:23-27]

85. Another tradition is that we are not to ex-

pect healing for certain afflictions; the scripture is quoted: *Is any among you afflicted? Let them pray.*[Ja.5:13] This again does not refer to sickness, but to the same thing pointed out in No. 82 and No. 84 above.

86. Another tradition is that God chastises His children with sickness. The favored scripture is in Hebrews, chapter twelve, verses six to eight, a part of which says, *Whom the Lord loves, he chastens.* This is true; God does chastise those He loves, but it does not say that He makes them sick. The word chastise in this instance means: To instruct, train, discipline, teach or educate; like a teacher instructs a pupil, or like a parent trains and teaches a child.

87. When a teacher instructs a student, various means of discipline are employed but never sickness. When a parent trains a child, different means of punishment are used. But never is physical disease put upon a child by a parent. For our heavenly Father to chastise or punish us does not require that He lay a disease upon us. Our diseases were laid upon Christ. God would not require that we bear, as punishment, what Jesus has borne for us. Christ's sacrifice freed us forever from the curse of sin and disease which He bore for us.

88. The most common tradition is that the day of miracles is past. (See Chapter 18 — Healing for

Today.) For this to be true, there would have to be a complete absence of miracles. Even one miracle would prove that the age of miracles is not past.

89. If the time of miracles were past, no one could be born again, because the new birth is the greatest miracle in the world.

90. If the epoch of miracles were past, as some claim, that would mean that all the technical evidence examined in hundreds of laboratories of the world, concerning innumerable cases of miraculous healings, is false.

91. Anyone who claims that the era of miracles is past denies the need, the privileges and the benefits of prayer. For God to hear and answer prayer, whether the petition is for a postage stamp or for the healing of a cripple, is a miracle. If prayer brings an answer, that constitutes a miracle.

If there are no miracles, then there is no reason for faith. If there are no miracles, then prayer is fraudulent, and only lack of intelligence could cause a person to pray, expecting an answer. When God answers prayer, that is a miracle.

Everyone who prays should expect an answer to their prayer. When that prayer is answered, God has performed something beyond the powers of nature or supernatural. That is a miracle. To disprove miracles today is to disfavor prayer today.

92. The epoch of miracles is not past, because the miracle worker remains the same. *Jesus Christ the same yesterday, and to day, and for ever.*[He.13:8]

93. When Jesus sent His disciples to preach the gospel, He told them *These* (supernatural) *signs shall follow them that believe.* This was for *every creature,* for *all nations,* until *the end of the world.*[Mk.16:15-17; Mt.28:19-20] The end of the world has not come yet, so the time of miracles has not passed. Christ's Commission has never been withdrawn or annulled.

94. Christ's promise for the soul, *shall be saved,* is in the Great Commission, and is for all. His promise for the body, *shall recover,* is in the Great Commission, and is for all. To deny that one part of Christ's command is for today is to deny that the other part is for today as well.

As long as the Great Commission is in effect, you can be healed spiritually and physically, by believing the gospel. Multiplied thousands of sincere people all over the world are receiving both physical and spiritual healing through their simple consistent faith in God's promises.

95. Christ bore your sins so that you may be forgiven. Eternal life is yours. When you claim this blessing, and confess it by faith, God makes it good in your life.

96. Christ bore your diseases so that you may be healed. Divine health is yours. When you claim this blessing, and confess it by faith, God manifests it in your body.

97. Like all of Christ's redemptive gifts, divine healing is received by simple faith alone, and upon being received, is to be consecrated for Christ's service and glory alone.

98. God is as willing to heal His friends, as He is to forgive His enemies. That is to say, when you were a sinner, God was willing to forgive you. Now that you are His child, He is certainly willing to heal you. He was merciful enough to forgive you when you were His enemy. And He is merciful enough to heal you, now that you are His friend.[Ro.8:32]

99. To be saved, you accept God's promise as true and believe that you are forgiven. Then you can experience the joy of spiritual healing. To be healed, you accept God's promise as true and believe you are healed. Then you can experience the joy of physical healing.

100. *As many* (sinners) *as received him were born of God.*[Jn.1:12-13] *As many* (sick) *as touched him were made whole.*[Mk.6:56]

When we say that it is always God's will to heal, the question is immediately raised: "How then could one ever die?"

The Bible says: *He takes away their breath, they die, and return to the dust.*[Ps.104:29] *You shall come to your grave in a full age, like a shock of corn comes in season.*[Jb.5:26]

For us to reach our *full age,* and for God to take away our breath, does not require the aid of a disease. God's will in the death of His child (or what we call death), is that, after we have lived a fruitful life, fulfilling the number of our days, that we simply stop breathing, and fall asleep in Christ, only to awake again in heaven and live with Him forever. *So shall we ever be with the Lord.*[1Th.4:17] Indeed, this is the hope of the righteous.[1Th.4:13; Ti.2:13; 1Pe.1:3]

Because you have set your love upon me, (God says), *I will deliver you: I will set you on high, because you have known my name. You shall call upon me, and I will answer you: I will be with you in trouble; I will deliver you, and honor you. With long life will I satisfy you, and show you my salvation.*[Ps.91:14-16]

PART

VI

PROSPERITY FOR GOD'S GLORY

WHEN I BEGAN TO SEE money from God's point of view, I discovered that God wills prosperity and material abundance for those who take Him as a partner.

The world of plenty all about you is ample proof that your heavenly Father wants you to live in His abundance.

God is not limited to your income, or farm, or salary, or business, or stocks, or securities, or pension, or interest. All wealth is His creation, and He has unlimited ways to place it into your hands for His glory.

The miracle of dollar bills that we experienced in our youth taught me that God can do material miracles as easily as the spiritual or physical. ➠

Chapter 20

The Key to Abundance

ONE OF THE MOST important aspects of the good life is the principle of sowing and reaping.

The apostle Paul said: Whatever you sow, that shall you also reap.[Ga.6:7]

In the beginning of time, God laid down a law that was never to be changed:

While the earth remains, seedtime and harvest shall not end.[Ge.8:22]

This principle of sowing or giving in order to reap and receive is one of the most basic fundamentals of the good life.

It all begins with the way God saves us.

God so loved that he gave.[Jn.3:16]

There can be no loving without giving.

There can be no giving without receiving.

There can be no planting without reaping.

Let us not love in word, neither in tongue; but in deed and in truth.[1Jn.3:18]

When we love in deed and action, we are planting seeds that will return to us a harvest in whatever form of love we expressed.

When we give, we are planting seeds that will be multiplied back to us.

When we plant, we are sowing seeds that will miraculously germinate and reproduce of their own kind in a bountifully increased measure.

It is impossible to love without being loved, to give without receiving, to plant without reaping.

Two principles are infallible:

1. We always reap the same kind of seed we plant.

2. We always reap more than we plant.

These laws are true in all aspects. They always have been and they always shall remain true.

Love and be loved.

Help and be helped.

Extend kindness and receive kindness.

Show mercy and receive mercy.

Give and receive more of whatever you give.

Sow and reap more of whatever you plant.

The story is told of a poor farmer who "jest play'd it safe!" He sat on the step of his tumble-down shack, clothed in rags, barefoot, desolate.

A stranger came by and stopped for a drink of water, and asked:

"How's your cotton comin' on?"

"Ain' got none," reflected the farmer.

"Did ye plant any?" asked the stranger.

"Nope." was the reply. "'Fraid o' boll weevils."

"Well," continued the visitor, "How's your corn?"

"Didn' plant none. 'Fraid there wasn't gonna be no rain."

"Well, how are your potatoes?"

"Ain' got none. Scairt o' potato bugs."

"Really? Well what did you plant, mister?" asked the stranger.

"Nothin'. I jest play'd it safe!"

To know a prosperous, happy, successful life, you first learn to plant.

Plant love, plant mercy, plant kindness, plant strength, plant faith, plant money, plant whatever good thing God has given to you, and you will reap an abundant return of the same blessing.

Chapter 21

Two Words that Changed Our Lives

THE GOOD LIFE of abundant living in Jesus Christ is a faith life. It is a life of trust in God. One comes to know that God *is and that he is a rewarder of them that diligently seek him.*[He.11:6]

To know that God is real, and that His promises in the Bible are trustworthy, you just put them to the test. Every person at some time in life, does this if their Christian experience is to be meaningful.

God knows this and He has specifically challenged us to prove Him. But this challenge has been issued on the most unexpected basis.

I shall never forget the day we learned this and it changed our lives. Since then, whenever we have been able to help anyone grasp this secret God revealed to us, happiness, health, success and prosperity has begun to fill their lives — and it will happen to you too.

We had an unusual experience with God during a personal financial crisis.

We had over-extended our evangelism commitments. Our big outreaches are planned far in advance. It sometimes takes months to negotiate large printing contracts and to get the paper shipped to the overseas printer; or to get tools dispatched and plow through all of the paperwork and red tape getting equipment cleared through customs offices; or to plan a campaign and tie all of the ends for a big gospel saturation.

So, we had committed ourselves to a whole spread of evangelism projects in several countries over a very brief period of time. Our commitments had been made months ahead. We moved by faith. We felt the needs were urgent. We saw the doors were open at the moment though they might not be for long, so we kept promising assistance.

Then, it seemed that these responsibilities began to come due all at once. We just did not have the funds available to meet the urgent needs.

On top of it all, we were ready to leave for another great crusade overseas. Fares had to be paid, equipment air freighted, plus all of the crusade expenses which had to be met.

It is times like that when Satan dishes out some heavy accusations like: "You think you have faith? You say you are doing the thing nearest God's heart? You talk about reaching the unreached and say God is depending on you? Now where is your God — and where are your partners? You quote scripture like: *Seek for the expansion of God's kingdom worldwide first, then all things are given to you.* But now, you see, that is not true. You have given priority to the unreached, but your God has abandoned you. He will not supply you this time."

Daisy and I chose to go away for one week to fast and pray and listen.

As we prayed and waited before God for His answer for us, I heard these words: "Prove me. Prove me now, the Lord says."

I knew where these words were in the Bible — and I knew they had to do with tithes and offerings.[Mal.3:10] But I did not relate these particular verses to our situation. I supposed there were many places in the Bible where God had told His people to prove Him.

So I began to search the Bible. I intended to list each scripture where God told His people to prove Him. I was going to organize them and see if I could discover a pattern by which God might clarify what He was saying to me.

What an amazing discovery I made.

In the Bible, **there is only one time when God ever called on His people to PROVE Him. And that concerned their MONEY.**

Money was our immediate problem.

We needed money for evangelism.

The only way we could fulfill evangelism commitments was with **money.**

To preach the gospel required **money.**

Our burden was a lack of **money.**

We were praying concerning **money.**

The devil had accused us about **money.** He had incriminated God of being unconcerned about souls because **money** was lacking.

So **money** was our problem.

Now God had spoken to me: **"Prove me. Prove me now."**

I had made the discovery that God said this about money.

That day our need and God's supply came into focus for the first time.

We realized: Christ gave the Great Commission. Then He assigned us and every Christian to carry it out. Some would *go;* Mk.16:15 others would *send.* Ro.10:15 I began to add it all up: People are His agents. People like you and me are involved. God chooses to use people.

God places us here on earth, owning nothing but our souls. **Then all of earth's things — possessions, houses, lands, money — are entrusted to us, as people, in order that God may prove us as His stewards.**

Then God says: *Bring your tithes and offerings* (your money) *and put me to the test.* His actual words: *Prove me now by this, if I will not open you the windows of heaven, and pour you out a blessing, that there shall not be room enough to receive it.*[Mal.3:10]

Then, for the farmer or rancher, He adds:

And I will rebuke the devourer for your sakes, and he shall not destroy the fruits of your ground; neither shall your vine cast her fruit before the time in the field.[Mal.3:11]

Notice that equal providence is extended to the one *in the city* or *in the field.*[De.28:3]

He tells us to bring our money (tithes and offerings or firstfruits) to Him and prove God as our only provider. In return, **He proves His covenant by opening the windows of heaven, returning to us more than He entrusted us with the first time, so that we, in turn, may bring back more to Him to prove God in a bigger way, and receive back again a bigger portion** — the object being to carry out His will on earth.

When I finally realized that the only time God ever asked us to put Him to the test was with our money, frankly I was astounded. **I had never in all of my Christian life regarded money with any spiritual significance.**

God was spiritual. Money was carnal, I thought. I had been poor all of my life. What I knew about money was what I had learned from religious people around me: that it was evil, that I should beware of it and never desire it, that the only way I could stay humble and submissive to God's will was to remain poor.

But that day in prayer, asking God to provide for the urgent needs of evangelism, I heard God say, "**Prove me. Prove me now.**"

Then I made that breathtaking discovery that **the only time God had ever told His people to prove Him, He had said to do it – with MONEY.**

It was the first time in my life to **see money as God sees it.**

Only God knows what could happen in getting the gospel to *every creature*[Mk.16:15] if every preacher, priest, teacher and lay Christian would exchange the religious view of money for God's idea and attitude about it.

You see, **money represents life.**

When you are paid a salary, that money represents the period of your life it took to earn it. You will never live that part of your life again. You will never earn that particular money again. Your salary represents **a portion of your life, in the form of currency.**

That is why your money is valued next to your life itself. It is your most treasured material possession. You instinctively guard it more than anything else, except your life.

Jesus said, *Where your treasure is, there will your heart be also.*[Lu.12:34]

Now you can understand why God says: *Bring your money to me and put me to the test with it.*

He is calling for the dearest temporal treasure you have – whether you are a millionaire or whether you are like the widow with only two mites.[Mk.12:42-44]

God is saying: **If you trust Me with your MONEY, you will trust Me with your LIFE. When you entrust your money to my hands, you are proving that you will trust me with your soul.**

From the beginning of time, people with faith in God have consecrated to Him the offerings of their best.[Ge.4:3-4; Ge.8:20; Ge.22:9-14; Ex.12:5; Le.22:21; Nu.18:12] The Bible calls it **firstfruits**[2Ch.31:5; Ne.10:35-37] – the **first** and the **best** for God's work.[Ex.22:29-30; Ex.23:19]

There can be little faith in God that does not touch one's money, because money represents life. What you do with your money is what you do with your life. **What you really believe in is proven by where you put your money.**[Mt.6:21]

This is why God's call to every one of His children is: **Prove your faith in Me by bringing your money to Me.** *Prove me now, with this, the Lord* *says.*

Then He states His covenant or pact:

I will pour you out a blessing (of so much more **money** than you brought to me) *that there will not be room enough to receive it.*[Mal.3:10]

You put money into God's work when you really believe in Him. That is why God says to bring Him your money and put Him to the test. And you will see what He will do in return.

When you put **your money** in God's work, **your heart** is in God's work because you put your money in what you really believe in. **Your money proves your faith.**

So God asks you to put Him to the test with your most treasured temporal possession, to prove that you trust Him for your most precious spiritual possession – your soul.[Mk.8:36-37]

Then He promises to return to you abundantly more than you trusted Him with, as proof that He is real and that His pact is valid.

Honor the Lord with your substance (temporal things), *and with the firstfruits* (the first and the best) *of all your increase: So shall your barns be filled with plenty.*[Pr.3:9-10]

God's law is to give Him your best – as proof of your faith in Him, putting Him and His word to the test. Then receive His abundance in return.

"Prove Me. Prove Me now," God says.

It is significant that He would speak those words to me when we were so burdened by the need for money.

That was when God's pact of plenty was born in my heart.

I saw His words:

PROVE ME NOW, THE LORD SAYS,

THAT YOU MAY PROSPER.

From that day, **I saw money from God's point of view.** I knew that I was to share this vital truth of Christian living with everyone.

We realized that some would criticize us for talking or writing about money. But they are generally those who *love their money* [1Ti.6:10] **too much to prove God with it.** Other times it has been those sincerely prejudiced about money by their religious tradition. They, themselves, never seriously attempted to share the gospel with the whole world — a mission that requires millions of dollars.

I knew that God could only confirm His pact of plenty through material miracles as people would exercise faith in His promises, and I knew that *faith comes* (only) *by hearing the word of God.* [Ro.10:17]

So I began a series of lessons **to teach the promises of God concerning money and wealth and**

prosperity. I want to help Christians accept **God's attitude about money** instead of guarding a biased and negative religious attitude.

I recognized that people must be taught God's will and material blessings. They can exercise their faith accordingly. God wants His people to see that *it is he who gives them power to get wealth.*[De.8:18] *Riches and wealth are the gift of God.*[Ec.5:19] *The Lord has pleasure in the prosperity of his servant.*[Ps.35:27] He wishes *above all things that you may prosper.*[3Jn.2]

So He says, *Bring your money and prove me with it. Put me to the test. See how I will open heaven and return a harvest greater than you sowed and your barns will overflow with plenty.*

When God spoke those words to me, I saw His **covenant of prosperity,** His **pact of plenty.**

I understood how **we plant by reaching out to others, then we reap as God reaches out to us.**[Lu.6:38]

There are three definite blessings guaranteed by God's pact of plenty to every Christian who becomes involved in His No. 1 Job of giving the gospel to others.

1) **All of your needs** – spiritual, physical and financial – fully supplied.

2) **Souls saved** every place that your seed-money is planted in evangelism.

3) **Financial prosperity** for you — the harvest of your seed-faith giving.

God promised that if you will honor Him with your firstfruits (your first and your best), that your barns shall be filled with plenty.[Pr.3:9-10] Set aside your firstfruits seed money each week. Then before you pay a single bill of your own, plant those firstfruits in God's No. 1 Job to prove that the Lord's work comes first in your life.

When you **put Him first** with your firstfruits, then you can **claim His best** in your life.

Put His covenant to the test and see for yourself. *There has not failed one word of all his good promise which he has promised.*[1Ki.8:56]

Chapter 22

Promises of Prosperity

GOD CREATED WOMAN and man for the good life.

It is not His will that we should live a life of sin and guilt, of disease and suffering, of failure and poverty. One is no more God's will than the other.

The entire Bible is God's revealed plan of complete and full salvation for the whole person, spiritually, physically and materially.

The good life of abundant living which God has so generously and mercifully granted us through Jesus Christ, includes every blessing and provision we can ever need or desire — so long as we accept Christ as Lord of our lives and strive to honor and serve Him in all that we think and say and do.

This gives us the right perspective in all of the spiritual, physical and material blessings we receive from God.

Blessed be the Lord, who daily loads us with benefits, even the God of our salvation. Ps.68:19

John the beloved apostle, who knew perhaps better than anyone else what the will of God is for all who believe on Christ, said:

Beloved, I wish above all things that you may prosper, and be in health even as your soul prospers.[3Jn.2]

That word *prosper,* in the original Greek, clearly includes financial abundance.

In order to receive God's material blessings by faith, 1) be convinced that it is God's will for you to prosper financially, and 2) be willing to accept the responsibility of good stewardship.[1Co.4:2; Lu.16:1-2; Lu.16:8-11; 1Pe.4:10; 1Ti.6:17-18]

God wills that you prosper in three ways according to the apostle John: 1) financially, 2) physically and 3) spiritually – prosperity for the whole person.

All the wealth of the world is created by our Father. The gold and the silver, the oil and the minerals, the precious stones and the fields, the flocks and the herds are all the creation of our Father. He owns it all.[Ex.19:5; Le.25:23; Ps.50:10-11; Hag.2:8]

We are just temporary stewards of the earth's wealth. God, our Father, is the permanent owner. When He needs it for His work, He has to adjust circumstances in order to put some of that wealth into our hands to use for His glory.

As a Christian, here are two basic facts of God's good life:

1. Your Father created all of the wealth on this earth and it is His. He can and will place it in your hands for His work's sake as you claim His promises and act upon them by faith.

2. Your Father wills that you share financial prosperity for His glory and for His work. Poverty is of the devil as much as sickness or oppression or any other thing that hinders or limits your personal happiness and your outreach for souls.

These two facts will affect your whole attitude about money.

God knows your height.[Lu.12:25] He has numbered the hairs of your head.[Mt.10:30] Every sparrow is counted,[Lu.12:6] and He is concerned about each need you have.[Ps.31:19; Is.64:4; Ph.4:19] He feeds the birds and clothes the lilies [Lu.12:27-28] and it is His will that you live in abundance.[Jn.10:10]

God's plan is for you to be saved, blessed, happy, healthy, prosperous, successful and wise. If it were sinful for you to enjoy material blessings, then God would not have created them nor promised that you may have them.

The world of plenty all about us is ample proof that our heavenly Father wants us to live in abundance. God created enough so that everyone can enjoy all that is needed or desired.

Can you imagine parents who do not wish good

and prosperity for their children? Could God be less loving and good than earthly parents?

If you then, being evil, know how to give good gifts to your children; how much more shall your heavenly Father give good things to them that ask him.[Mt.7:11]

Religious tradition often seems to infer that it is God's will for His people to be poor, helpless, defeated, crushed and sorrowful. Is it necessary to live in poverty in order to stay humble and godly? Are we supposed to be subject to defeat and powerless to avoid sin, sickness and failure in order to avoid pride and rebellion? Does God teach us patience, humility and submission with pain, physical suffering and poverty?

The average Christian holds a limited concept of God, whose resources have never yet been fully tapped. Through this lesson, I hope you can see for yourself the abundance of God's provision for you.

The facts of the Bible are that God has promised and provided spiritual freedom from sin and the consequences of the sinful nature. He has promised physical health and soundness as well as material wealth, success and plenty. There can be no failure in life for anyone who taps the unlimited and abundant resources of God.

All of the wealth of this planet was created by our heavenly Father. It is good. He provided it — not for unbelievers to monopolize, but for the prosperity and material blessing of His children who do His will.

Money and material prosperity are blessings that God wills for His children, so that they can be partners with Him in His No. 1 Job of giving the gospel to others.

The scriptures promise us all that is good and that contributes to happiness and contentment and joy. God is good, and He wills good things for you.

Part of God's blessing which He covenants to give to all who *listen to the Lord* is that He *shall make you plenteous in goods.*[De.28:1, 11]

It comes as a shock to many to realize that Jesus spoke more about money than He did about heaven or hell.

God has promised abundant living — the good life.

Jesus came *that you might have life and that you might be in abundance.*[Jn.10:10 FB]

It seems almost incredible that religious tradition could overlook so many promises of material prosperity for those who are committed to carrying out God's will on earth. Our top priority on earth is to give the message of Jesus to *every creature.* That demands money. That is why God wills that we prosper.

Riches and wealth are the gift of God.[Ec.5:19]

Blessed is the one who fears the Lord, who delights in his commandments. Wealth and riches shall be in their house.[Ps.112:1, 3]

The Lord has pleasure in the prosperity of his servants.[Ps.35:27] That means you — and it means financial prosperity.

No good thing will he withhold from them that walk uprightly.[Ps.84:11]

That I may cause those that love me to inherit substance; and I will fill their treasures.[Pr.8:21]

Observe to do according to (My word) *that you may prosper wherever you go.*[Jos.1:7]

Keep the words of this covenant, that you may prosper in all that you do.[De.29:9]

Walk in God's ways,so that you may prosper in all that you do, and wherever you turn yourself.[1Ki.2:3]

The Lord shall make you plenteous in goods.[De.28:11]

The blessing of the Lord, it makes rich.[Pr.10:22]

The Lord is my shepherd, I shall not want.[Ps.23:1]

They that seek the Lord shall not want any good thing.[Ps.34:10]

Blessed be the Lord, who daily loads us with benefits.[Ps.68:19]

Seek first the kingdom of God (the expansion of God's kingdom worldwide) *and all these things shall be added to you.*[Mt.6:33 RV]

He wills *that you may prosper wherever you go, that you make your way prosperous, and that you have good success.*[Jos.1:5-9]

The Lord shall make you prosperous in goods. The Lord shall open to you his good treasure, to bless all the work of your hand.[De.28:11-12]

You shall eat in plenty and be satisfied and praise the name of the Lord your God, that has dealt wondrously with you.[Jl.2:26]

God has given riches and wealth and power to rejoice in your labor; this is the gift of God.[Ec.5:19]

Let the Lord be magnified, which has pleasure in the prosperity of his servants.[Ps.35:27]

Wealth and riches shall be in your house.[Ps.112:1, 3]

With you is the fountain (source) *of life.*[Ps.36:9]

The Lord makes poor, and makes rich.[1S.2:7]

Both riches and honor come of you.[1Ch.29:12]

O Lord, the earth is full of your riches.[Ps.104:24]

Believe in the Lord your God, so shall you prosper.[2Ch.20:20]

Those that seek me early shall find me. Riches and honor are with them.[Pr.8:17-18]

The wealth of the earth is our Father's. *The silver is mine, and the gold is mine.*[Hag.2:8] *All the earth is mine.*[Ex.19:5] *The land is mine.*[Le.25:23] *Every beast of the forest is mine, and the cattle on a thousand hills.*[Ps.50:10]

God warned against attributing prosperity to one's own skill or business ability. He clearly showed that His will is for His children to inherit *good land, to eat good things, to build goodly houses; for your herds and flocks to multiply and your silver and gold to be multiplied.*[De.8:7-13] This is His will for you.

But then He warned: *Beware that you forget not the Lord and say in your heart, my power and the might of my hand has gotten me this wealth.*[De.8:11, 17]

God said in unmistakable terms:

Remember the Lord your God: For it is he that gives you power to get wealth.[De.8:18]

He said, *Honor the Lord with the firstfruits of all your increase: So shall your barns be filled with plenty.*[Pro.3:9-10]

God says to bring your tithes and offerings to Him and *prove me now with this, if I will not open you the windows of heaven, and pour you out a blessing that there shall not be room enough to receive it.*[Mal.3:10]

Jesus said, *There is no one that has left house, or brothers, or sisters, or father, or mother, or wife, or children, or lands, for my sake, and the gospel's, but they shall receive an hundredfold now in this life and in the world to come eternal life.*[Mk.10:29-30]

Jesus said: *Give, and it shall be given to you: good measure, pressed down, and shaken together, and run-*

ning over. For with the same measure that you use to give it shall be used to measure to you again.[Lu.6:38]

Give and it shall be given to you is as absolute as, *Ask and you shall receive.*[Jn.16:24]

All the promises of God are yes and amen.[2Co.1:20]

God created an abundance of everything. He placed us here amidst it all. He is rich. He receives us when we receive Christ. He wills that we enjoy His plenty — spiritually, physically and materially.

There are innumerable scriptures that tell us that God wants His children to prosper and to be blessed materially so long as our motive is right.

God is able to give you everything you need and more, so that there will not only be enough for your own needs, but plenty left over to give joyfully to others.

For God, who gives to the farmer to plant, and later on, good crops to harvest and eat, will give you more and more seed to plant and will make it grow so that you can give away more and more fruit from your harvest.

Yes, God will give you much so that you can give away much, and when you take your gifts to those who need them they will break out into thanksgiving and praise to God for your help.[2Co.9:10-11 LB]

My God shall supply all your needs.[Ph.4:19]

For God to supply all your needs, He must provide money. You must have money to meet your own needs and then to carry out God's will on earth. You are learning the secret of God's financial as well as His spiritual and physical blessings.

God is good, and He wills to manifest His goodness toward you. *I will rejoice over them to do them good with my whole heart and with my whole soul* [Je.32:41] – and our God has a very big heart and a very big soul.

Chapter 23

Getting God's Attitude About Money

TO ACCOMPLISH GOD'S No. 1 Job on earth – that of giving the gospel to *every creature,* we need to get rid of the religious tradition that money is evil, and that poverty is sacred.

Money is not evil. The love of money is the root of all evil.[1Ti.6:10]

Riches and wealth are the gift of God.[Ec.5:19]

Jesus said to seek first the expansion of God's kingdom worldwide, and all of these things shall be added to you.[Mt.6:33 RV]

You see, God promised to meet all of your needs when you serve His purpose and carry out His will.

My God shall supply all your needs according to his riches in glory by Christ Jesus.[Ph.4:19]

No good thing will he withhold from them that walk uprightly before him.[Ps.84:11]

Jesus promised: Whatever things you desire, when you pray, believe that you receive them, and you shall have them.[Mk.11:24]

For your own needs to be met, you need money. For God to supply all of your needs, He will help you to acquire money. He did it as recorded in the Bible. He will do it today.

The Bible teaches that God has never changed.[Mal.3:6] He is the great I am.[Ex.3:14-15] Jesus Christ is the same yesterday, and to day and for ever.[He.13:8]

If you could read the prayer requests that come to us in the mail, you would understand that people have many material needs — that cost money.

People from all over the world write to us and request prayer that God will provide money to pay their bills, that they can get a car, or buy a house, or rent an apartment. They want a job, or better clothes, or a better business.

They need money for a trip, a business venture, industrial or business tools; for repairs on their house or car or equipment.

They request prayer that God will intervene in their financial need for medicine, hospital care, dental work, glasses; for cattle, sheep, poultry or other farm animals; for crop planting, cultivating, disinfesting or harvesting; for repairs or new ventures; for funds to move from one place to another; for a train trip or for gasoline — and a thousand and one other material needs.

They ask us to pray for these needs. We do pray for these things and our daily mail bears abundant evidence that God answers prayer and meets material needs — often by unexplainable miracles.[Je.32:17, 27; Lu.18:27]

Aside from the spiritual needs of people, most of their needs require money. Things cost money. God created all the wealth of this earth — not for unbelievers to monopolize, but for the prosperity of His children who do His will. So God is interested in your temporal and material needs too.

The Bible contains innumerable promises for financial and material prosperity. But too often we hear only the negative side of the subject:

That the love of money is the root of all evil.[1Ti.6:10]

That they that love silver shall not be satisfied with silver.[Ec.5:10]

That it is hard for them that trust in riches to enter the kingdom of God.[Mk.10:24]

That the rich man rejected Jesus and was very sorrowful: for he was very rich.[Lu.18:23]

That they that trust in riches shall fall.[Pr.11:28]

That they that will be rich will fall into temptation and a snare, and into many foolish and hurtful lusts, which drown them in destruction and perdition.[1Ti.6:9]

That riches are deceitful.[Mt.13:22]

These and many other scriptures constitute the negative side of the subject — and these admonitions should be carefully heeded.

But to get God's perspective of money, we need to understand that money in itself is not evil. It is the love of money that is the root of all evil.

While God never intended that His people live in poverty, neither did He intend that they set their heart on the things of this world.[Co.3:1-2; 1Jn.2:15-17]

We are consistently warned to not trust in uncertain riches[1Ti.6:6-7, 17] and if riches increase, set not your heart upon them.[Ps.62:10] This is why Jesus emphasized how hard it is for them that trust in riches to enter the kingdom of God.[Mk.10:24] We are to trust in God.[Ps.37:3; Ps.73:28; Ps.91:2; Ps.115:11-12; Pr.3:5]

When you trust in wealth,[Ps.20:7] you fail to see your need to trust in God. Your whole perspective becomes distorted by the false security of uncertain riches which can be so easily wiped out.

This was the big point which Saint Francis of Assisi felt compelled to demonstrate by his lifelong vow of poverty. He lived in an epoch of wealthy arrogance and ruthless dominance by the rich over the poor. Saint Francis made his unusual vow before God to live in such a way as to show the world that there was something more valuable than gold. And he made an indelible impact upon the world.

God did not demand this of Saint Francis. He did it out of his own intense love for God.

When greed, lust and envy motivate your pursuit of riches and your use of them, there is no doubt but that you will eventually weep and howl for the miseries that come upon you, as James said. Your riches are corrupted, and your garments are moth eaten. Your gold and silver is cankered; and the rust of them shall be a witness against you, and shall eat your flesh as it were fire.[Ja.5:1-3]

Christ said to the man who laid up treasure for himself, and was not rich toward God, You fool, this night your soul shall be required of you: then whose shall those things be, which you have provided?[Lu.12:20-21]

It is true that financial blessings cause some people to turn away from God, but their motives were wrong. Perhaps they would have forsaken God anyway. Just because some abandon their faith, trusting in their riches, should we blame the abundant love and providence of God?

There are people who turn away from God and sin by their obesity[De.21:20; Pr.23:1-2,21; Ph.3:18-19; Lu.12:19-20] or by the way they dress.[Lu.16:19; 1S.16:7; 1Pe.3:3-4 RV; Jn.7:24] One can be as full of pride over good clothes and a new car as over riches. But we should not condemn good food or clothing or automobiles or nice homes because some folks who acquire them forsake their trust in God.

Should we argue that these things are evil because they affect some people adversely? Neither should we argue that prosperity, health and abundant blessings are evil because some people who have these blessings do not serve God.

The devil's strategy is to promote accusing ideas about God's abundant providence and convince people that prosperity is evil, that poverty and suffering is godliness, so that millions would reject God.

Any Christian realizes that one must be alert to the potential negative aspect of either physical or financial blessings — or even spiritual arrogance.

Some people have a terrible spiritual pride. They count themselves holier than anyone else and constantly judge others.[Co.2:18; 2Pe.2:18] This is spiritual sin.

Others are proud of their health and of their attractive physiques, looking with contempt and scorn on others who are less robust or charming.[Ga.5:26; Co.2:8; Ph.2:3-8]

Some people flaunt their riches. They are haughty and high-minded, regarding the poor and miserable with disdain.[Pr.21:24; Pr.26:12; Ro.12:16; Ja.4:6]

This also is evil.

But these sinful attitudes do not mean that the blessings of salvation, health and prosperity are evil.

Among all of the promises and provisions of salvation, ecclesiastical tradition generally opposes only two of them: 1) Physical, miraculous healing and 2) financial, material prosperity.

Both of these blessings are clearly part of the good life which God wills for you. He wants you to enjoy both in abundance.

Theologians have been known to limit God's power to spiritual miracles. They readily admit that anyone can be spiritually reborn. But they often reject the idea that God will do physical miracles such as healing the body. The idea that God would meet material needs by a miracle would usually be considered ridiculous.

God's power is not limited to spiritual things. He wills to also supply our physical and our material needs. He desires to manifest His miracle power in the physical and material realms as well as in the spiritual realm.

It was never God's will for His children to live under the curse of poverty, need and failure.

Religious tradition presents us a strange philosophy. It tells us that God made all of the gold and the silver in the earth, that it is the creation of

His own word from the beginning. Yet we are led to believe that only the unconverted should possess that wealth — that Christians should be poor in order to remain humble and submissive.

Is it not strange how we overlook scriptures if they conflict with tradition? In Chapter 20 we have given many scriptures which clearly contradict the theory of poverty for the believer.

To say that money, wealth and prosperity will make you carnal and proud is like saying life, health and happiness will make you evil-minded and carnal.

Should only the unconverted possess God's wealth?

To believe that only the unconverted should prosper is like believing that only the unconverted should have life and health.

But poverty has been so eulogized that many good Christians do not allow themselves to consider prosperity. They are persuaded that they might backslide, or become proud, or wasteful, or arrogant if they were blessed materially. So they live under the bondage of poverty and never become partners with God like He designed them to be.

This attitude is a vain tradition, making the word of God of no effect,[*Mk.7:13*] concerning God's financial blessings. Be convinced that it is God's will, that He wants you to prosper – for His work's sake and for His glory. Then learn success principles and act upon them with faith that God wills prosperity. And never quit.[1Ti.6:12]

Traditional religion around the world has, as a general rule, taught that to be spiritual or holy or humble, one should live in poverty, suffering and discomfort; and that if one is blessed materially, they are apt to be proud, merciless, wicked and ungodly.

While this has often happened, it is also true that some of the most cruel and ungodly people on earth are on the poverty level, stealing, killing, destroying and hating in their pursuit of money. While not all prosperous people are generous and kind, it is true that some of the most gentle, benevolent and loving people on earth are materially wealthy, giving, sharing, loving and spreading kindness wherever they can help people.

This must be why Agur prayed: *Remove far from me vanity and lies: Give me neither poverty nor riches; feed me with food convenient for me: lest I be full, and deny You, and say, Who is Lord? or lest I be poor, and steal, and take the name of your God in vain.*[Pr.30:8-9]

It is a fact that either riches or poverty can be evil, depending on our attitude. It is also clear that if God's No. 1 Job is ever to be accomplished, there must be Christians on whom God can bestow the responsibility of good stewardship, for

His glory.

We must learn to receive God's blessings graciously and utilize them for the good of others, and avoid the temptations of sinful pride and of the unholy use of them. It is the right use of God's blessings that is important.

Many people say, "I'd rather be poor and stay humble and spiritual. If I get money, I may become proud and carnal." Do you think so?

Here, I believe, is where tradition has laid its most cunning roadblock.

Christians have been so convinced that poverty and limited means are a virtue that thousands of them actually believe their poverty is a blessing. They are convinced in themselves that it would be sinful to be blessed financially. They would never dream of studying and believing God to lead them into real financial prosperity for His work.

Satan uses many cunning devices [2Co.2:11] to misguide people about money. He constantly glorifies poverty and praises those who are poor. He accuses those who prosper of being proud and haughty. He applauds the poor and boasts of their humility. He extols them for their humble insufficiency. He distorts scriptures to condemn anyone who prospers, and to praise anyone who is poor.

It is all a tool of Satan to limit the spread of the gospel.

The whole Christian value of financial prosperity rests on one's attitude toward money, and one's objective in its use.

If you love money and covet it to hoard, and if you trust in riches [*Mk.10:24*] or set your heart on money,[*Ps.62:10*] this is evil and wrong and will only prove to be a snare, for miseries shall come upon you as your gold and silver is cankered; and the rust of them shall witness against you.[*Ja.5:1-3*]

But when you look upon money as a personal blessing, as a tool for evangelism, and as a means to obey our Lord's last command to give the gospel to every creature; when you enter a faith partnership with God to prosper financially in order to live in the abundance Jesus came to share with you,[*Jn.10:10*] and to be able to send the gospel into all the world, you can be sure that God's will is to bless you with His material abundance and goodness.

Chapter 24

God will be Your Partner

ONE OF THE GREATEST discoveries in the good life with Christ is to learn how to sow money for God's glory and how to become a business partner with Him in order to share in carrying out His No. 1 Job — giving the gospel to those who have not yet received it.

Paul said: When someone becomes a Christian that person becomes brand new inside. A new life has begun and God has given them the privilege of urging everyone to be reconciled to him. This is the wonderful message he has given us to tell others. We are Christ's ambassadors.[2Co.5:17-20 LB]

Jesus plainly said, Follow after me and I will make you to become fishers of people.[Mt.4:19]

He said: The good news will be preached throughout the whole world, so that all nations will hear it.[Mt.24:14 LB] This is your opportunity to tell the good news. And the good news must first be made known in every nation.[Mk.13:9-10 LB]

His last instructions were: Go into all the world and preach the gospel to every creature.[Mk.16:15]

When Christ promised that every believer would receive the power of the Holy Ghost, the reason was to accomplish this task.

Jesus said: You shall receive power after the Holy Ghost is come on you. And you shall be my witnesses to the uttermost part of the earth.*Ac.1:8*

Our motto shall always be:

ONE WAY – ONE JOB.

The ONE WAY is Jesus.

The ONE JOB is Evangelism.

The supreme joy of every Christian is to give the gospel to every creature.

God loved the whole world.

Jesus died for the whole world.

Our greatest opportunity for success in life is to tell the good news to the whole world.

Jesus said: You go to the whole world.

So every Christian can either go or send the good news to others, and do both whenever possible.

Paul made an interesting resume of the Christian's objective in life:

Anyone who calls on the name of the Lord will be saved. But how shall they ask him to save them unless they believe in him? And how can they hear about him unless someone tells them?

And how will anyone go and tell them unless someone sends them? *Ro.10:13-15 LB*

So this, I say, is the honor of Christian living. We are saved to save others. Other Christians sacrificed to give us the gospel. Now it is our privilege to share it with others — either to GO or to SEND the good news — or to do both.

I shall never forget the day God spoke to me about reaching others with the gospel. Being just a poor lad on the farm, I was surely the most unlikely person on earth to be God's representative.

If you would have talked to me about reaching people in Tokyo or Paris or Buenos Aires, you might just as well have mentioned Jupiter, Mars or Venus. Those cities were like other planets to me.

But I believed the Bible. I believed in prayer. I believed in miracles. And God did the rest. For decades we have been involved in soulwinning on a large scale in practically every free nation on earth.

For many years we have sponsored as many as 2000 national preachers every month, as fulltime missionaries to unreached areas.

Year after year, we have published over a ton of literature per day, in 132 languages.

We have produced documentary films of our mass crusades in over 60 languages in both 16mm and Super-8 and have provided them free for evangelism worldwide, plus releasing them via mass media.

We have produced and provided our sermon tapes and cassettes in 70 languages and have furnished thousands of tape and cassette players, all free, to missions abroad.

We have provided over 100 mobile vans for evangelism on mission fields — all of this in addition to our mass evangelism crusades around the world.

Who could ever have dreamed that Daisy and I would have been chosen of God for such a world ministry. It has happened because we believe evangelism is God's No. 1 Job and that God will financially bless and prosper any Christian who takes part in such a ministry. That is why it is so important for Christians to learn the secrets of God's financial prosperity.

Satan will oppose every morsel of Bible truth about this subject because this is the greatest threat to his kingdom. As long as Christians remain in poverty and glorify God for their humble estate, believing it is for their good, to keep them submissive and holy, the gospel will never be preached to every creature. And until this is done, Christ cannot return.[*Mt.24:14*] Then Satan can continue his rule as the prince of this world.[*Jn.12:31; Jn.14:30; Ep.6:12*]

Once you learn how to plant money as seed in the fertile soil of God's No. 1 Job and once you realize how He will multiply it back to you in an increased measure according to His abundant promises, you will be amazed at how rapidly and miraculously God will bless you with His material goodness. Your life will become productive in God's will and you will discover God's abundance in the good life He has given to you in Jesus Christ.

God wants you to see yourself as a partner with Him — a financial partner; one in whose care He can trust His wealth in a flowing interchange of giving and receiving.

God wants you to see that giving and receiving links your act of faith with His unlimited supply and His infallible law of sowing and reaping.

When you invest your money in the Lord's work, it is seed-money planted in the soil of His divine will. Once planted in faith, it must reproduce itself and return to you a multiplied harvest of much more than you sowed. As sure as wheat seed yields more wheat, your firstfruits seed-money will yield more money.

When you give, you will receive more. Jesus said, Good measure, pressed down, and shaken together [*Lu.6:38*] — that is an abundant return. God's pact of plenty cannot fail.

A farmer sows seed before reaping a harvest.

The only seed that can be multiplied back is the seed that is planted. It is the same in God's law of giving and receiving. Only the seed-money which you plant in the Lord's work can be multiplied back in a harvest of financial prosperity.

Suppose a farmer gathered the family around and complained: "Why does God require me to give this good seed to the earth? Can He not see that my family needs this seed for food? I shall feed my children first. Our needs must be met first. If no seed remains, we shall believe for a miracle- harvest anyway. God can give us a harvest without requiring us to sow our seed because He knows we need it."

But that is what God will not do. He has ordained that there shall be no harvest if seed has not been sown.

The successful farmer sets aside the choice grain, the firstfruits, and gives it back to the earth. In return, the earth gives back an abundance of the same kind of seed that was sown. The barns are filled with plenty.[Pr.3:9-10] Thus, there is more to sow on greater fields.

The principle of giving which Jesus taught [Lu.6:38] is superior to the Old Testament law of tithing.[Le.27:30] Giving is the New Testament way of life.[Mk.10:29-30] It is as natural to a Christian as breathing. You give your time, talents, energies, your body, mind and money — your total life.

The more you give the more you receive, but giving comes first.

In tithing, you return ten percent of your earning to God after God has given to you one hundred percent. You do it more as a debt owed to God — a release of one-tenth of your money which you do not really consider your own. So you fulfill your obligation and return to God His tithe which is, in effect, a thanksgiving of ten percent, but only after you have received your full portion first.

But seed-giving is sowing. It is investing in the greatest security on earth — the unfailing covenant of God's prosperity which guarantees that every seed sown will reproduce itself in a multiplied return. But giving always comes first. This expresses faith in action.

Chapter 25

Expect a Good Harvest

THERE ARE SOME very important facts of sowing and reaping which are basic to the good life.

Jesus taught that every promise He gave was a seed. He said: *The seed is the word of God.*[Lu.8:11] That seed of His promise is *incorruptible* [1Pe.1:23] (undecaying, immortal, imperishable). The life in each seed of God's promise cannot die, or decay, or perish. God's seed-promises cannot fail.

As sure as wheat seed reproduces wheat, God's promises reproduce what they talk about for the person who plants them in the soil of His own believing heart.

It is impossible for a farmer to plant one kernel and to reap only one kernel. The reaper's return is always abundantly more than the sower planted.

This principle is true in all aspects of life. Jesus underscored its application to giving one day when He said, *It is more blessed to give than to receive.*[Ac.20:35] His point was that *it is more productive to give than to receive,* because only what you give is multiplied back to you again.

God's principle of sowing and reaping is the key to Christ's immortal statement about giving and receiving.

It is *more productive* for a farmer to sow grain seed (to give it to the earth) than to feed the family with it. By withholding the seed, the family may eat for awhile — but then they may die of starvation.

By giving that same seed to the earth, God's law of sowing and reaping guarantees an abundant return to the farmer of more than was sown.

One of the greatest hindrances to carrying out God's work is the tradition which says to give and to expect nothing in return. This is exactly opposite to God's law of sowing and reaping.

Many times I have heard Christians say: "Oh, I give because I want to give. I expect nothing in return."

Suppose a farmer said: "I sow my fields each spring because I just love to plant seed, but I expect nothing in return — no harvest." How long could the farmer survive?

The wise farmer expects a good harvest. Good seed always produces a multiplied return. It is God's will for you to reap more than you sow.

Each time you set aside your *firstfruits,* remember three basic points in planting your seed-money in the Lord's work.

FIRST: Keep your expectations only on the Lord. He alone is your supply – your only source. *God shall supply all of your need.*[Ph.4:19] Look only to Him. He is the life of every good seed. He is the creator of all wealth. He is the source from which your abundant return flows.

When you plant the seed-money of your *first-fruits* and anticipate your increased harvest, do not limit that source of increase to your employer's willingness to raise your salary, or to an increased interest or dividend on your savings or securities, or to any of the usual channels of income.

God is the source of your supply. Trust Him to give an abundant harvest in His own way. He may use these means I have mentioned, but He is not limited to them. He may perform a material miracle to prove His pact to you. The point is that you must keep your eye on Him – not on the means He might use. He, and He alone, is the source of your expectations.

SECOND: When you plant the seed-money of your *firstfruits* in the Lord's work, remember to plant for a harvest. Plant with an abundant return in mind. In other words, give objectively.

Give that the gospel may be preached. Give as a partaker in evangelism, but also – give so that you may receive more back again.

A farmer cannot afford to plant seed just because it gives a certain satisfaction. They plant seed to reap a harvest.

You cannot afford to give your money because you get a blessing out of giving. Your giving must be productive. If your giving does not produce a return of more than you give, how will evangelism be financed tomorrow?

Millions are still unconverted, and there will be millions more tomorrow. Give so that Christ's promise may be fulfilled — so that it may be given back to you for greater sowing and greater reaping.

Give so that God's covenant may be confirmed — so that you may prove God who declares that He will open heaven and overflow your barns.

Every time you sow or invest your *firstfruits* in the Lord's work, you are planting seed-money. Do it so that you may reap more than you give. Why? So that you may sow more seed the next time and reap an even greater harvest.

This is Christian stewardship.

This takes vision and demands faith. This calls for action and believing. This is why tradition has developed the easier way of keeping and losing — and dying, while millions are untouched for Christ.

God will help you to understand the glorious kingdom principle of giving and receiving so that

His gospel may be published throughout all the earth.

THIRD: When you sow your *firstfruits* as seed-money in God's work, expect a financial harvest. Expect a miracle.

In other words, plant your seed-money with faith.

Exercise faith that God will return more than you plant.

Expect God to fulfill His promise. Expect divine intervention to return to you more than you gave. Expect God to make His word good.

Without faith it is impossible to please him, for they that come to God must believe that he is and that he is a rewarder of them that diligently seek him.[He.11:6]

There can be no miracle without expectation. After farmers sow the seed, they expect growth. They exercise faith. If something delays the sprouting of the seed, you will see them checking their fields daily, lifting the soil, expecting.

After you have sown the seed-money of your *firstfruits,* expect growth. And keep your expectations in God as your only source because, as Paul said, *God gives the increase.*[1Co.3:6]

Once you have acted in faith on His word of promise, you have every right to expect a miracle return. You sowed. You expect to reap. Without expectation, faith is dead.

This is why we are on our knees every morning, praying and believing with each Christian partner in this vast world ministry. We are expecting and claiming what we know is God's will for each one of them — that their needs be met miraculously, and that they receive back a harvest of more than they planted in God's work.

This is the confidence that we have in him, that, if we ask anything according to his will (His word of promise is His will), *we know that we have the petitions that we desired of him.*[1Jn.5:14-15]

Every time a Christian partner's *firstfruits* are received for God's work, that is evidence on which to base faith for a financial harvest. That gift is planted as seed-money in the fertile soil of doing God's will. That planted seed will produce a harvest. God's law of sowing and reaping is unalterable. His pact of plenty is unfailing.

Believe that God wants you to be blessed financially as well as spiritually.[3Jn.2]

God wants you to be blessed by His material goodness as well as His spiritual and physical goodness. God created you for abundance, for good living.

Only when you are blessed, can you bless others. Only when you are lifted, can you lift others.

It is God's will that *riches and wealth*[Ps.112:1, 3] be in your house, that you drive a nice car, live in a nice home, dress and live like the child of divine royalty that you are. Then you can be God's partner in reaching, blessing and lifting others.

His will for you is always the good life.

Chapter 26

The Miracle of Dollar Bills

ONE OF THE GREAT discoveries for young Christians is to realize that wealth is of God and that He wills for them to prosper for His work's sake. This is the basis for faith to get wealth for your life, and to carry out His will on earth.

Then, after you make that discovery, you must act your faith.

To put faith into action is the secret to the fulfillment of all of God's promises.[Ja.2:14-17, 26]

1st: God gives the promise.

2nd: We hear it, believe it, and accept it as God's will.

3rd: We ask God to fulfill it.

4th: We act on the word of promise, proving by our action that we believe God will do as He promised.

5th: God sees our action which justifies our faith before Him, and He steps into the scene to fulfill His promise.

6th: Satan, God's enemy and our adversary,

steps in also, to create doubt, fear, confusion or hesitation in order to delay or prevent God's fulfillment and our joy.

7th: As our faith remains unwavering under trial, God's covenant cannot fail and He makes His word good, for *He watches over his words to perform them.*[Je.1:12] *No word from God is void of power.*[Lu.1:37 RV] *His covenant will he not break nor alter what has gone out of his lips,*[Ps.89:34] *for the scripture cannot be broken,*[Jn.10:35] and *heaven and earth shall pass away but my word shall never pass away.*[Mk.13:31]

So, upon the rock of God's promises which reveal His will, you, as a partner in soulwinning can step out by faith to become a co-worker with God in claiming His prosperity for your house and to give the gospel to others.

God always commands that we act our faith first. That proves our believing. Then, He steps into the scene to make good His promise.

A woman in the Bible was in debt and her creditors were coming to take her sons as bond servants. The prophet ordered her to act her faith. She borrowed many empty vessels, then took the only pot of oil she had and began sharing it. That was her faith in action. Her oil never failed and she was miraculously put into a thriving oil business that prospered so well that every debt was paid in full and she was told: *Live, you and your children of the rest.*[2K.4:1-7]

God does not need an oil well to put you into the oil business, or a larger farm to increase your supply of meal.

God is not limited to your income, or farm, or salary, or business, or stocks, or securities, or pension or interest.

All wealth is His creation. Act on His word. Claim His fulfillment. He has a million ways to place wealth into your hands.

God can do material miracles as easily as spiritual or physical ones.

Who can explain how God saves a sinner or heals a blind man? Is He limited to reasonable means? No. Neither is He limited in giving to you financial prosperity. I could recount hundreds of remarkable ways God has prospered Christians who have stepped by faith into an enlarged ministry of giving.

Those who may not understand this principle frown upon someone who gives out of a meager supply for the Lord's work. They forget Jesus' commendation of the widow who gave her last mite into the treasury.[*Mk.12:41-44*]

Daisy and I have always practiced this principle of seed-giving. I remember a time of dire financial need when we were young. Daisy did not have a coat. It was rainy, fall weather in California and our first child would soon be born. We attended a conference where the urgent need of a large missionary printing press was presented.

Before that conference ended, we borrowed a hundred dollars and planted it as seed-money in the Lord's work.

Very soon we were reaping an abundant return from that seed-gift. A woman bought my wife a beautiful new coat. A man presented us the title to an automobile. Money came from unexpected sources. God's law did not fail.

Another time, our faith was tested. We had purchased a new car and planned to pay for it through monthly installments. But that particular month we had given everything we had received. Whenever we saw an opportunity to win more souls, we planted our seed-money. We believed that the more we planted, the larger return we could claim. Our needs were large, so we planted liberally.

Our car payment was due. We lacked fourteen dollars. We had sown our seed-money, so we were believing for God's miracle supply. We prayed earnestly for God to meet our need. We claimed His covenant of prosperity. We knew the seed-dollars which we had sown must produce an increased return — even if God had to perform a material miracle. We were proving God — putting Him to the test as He said to do.[*Mal.3:10*]

We locked the door of our small room and went

to bed. No one knew our need but God alone. What happened that night may sound incredible, but God performed a material miracle to prove His pact of plenty in our lives.

When we awoke, one-dollar bills were scattered all over that room, as though they had literally been dropped from heaven, fluttering down onto the bed, the floor, behind the table and under the couch. We gathered up the dollar bills as reverently as the children of Israel gathered the manna from heaven,[Ex.16:14-18; Jn.6:31] or as the disciples gathered the fragments of bread and fish which Christ had multiplied.[Jn.6:12-13]

We looked in every nook and cranny of that room, and when we had gathered the last bill we could find, we counted them. There were exactly fourteen – the amount we needed to meet our obligation on time.

How glad we were that we had given our seed-money. We had sown dollars. Now we were reaping them. And before that month ended, our harvest was abundantly more than we had sown.

When Elijah visited the widow at Zarephath during the famine, she was destitute, preparing to cook her last cake of meal, then she and her son planned to die.

Elijah directed her to bake him a cake first. This seemed cruel and heartless. But when she obeyed, it was like a farmer planting his choice seed. That last cake became her seedcake. It produced an abundant return of much more than she gave to Elijah. *Her barrel diminished not, and her cruse of oil did not fail.*[1K.17:11-16]

PART

VII

THE CHURCH AND ITS FAITH

WE PROVE OUR LOVE for God best when we express His love toward others. We serve God best when we serve others in need.

Do not be confused by the multiplicity of doctrines. If true Christianity was as complex as some would make it seem to be, ordinary folks could never be saved.

You cannot lose your way when you follow Christ.

You serve Him best when you allow Him to love through you, when you let Him see human needs through your eyes, when you let Him care about those needs through your heart of love, when you let Him prove that love through your hands and feet and arms and all that you are and do. ➠

Chapter 27

The Value of Good Company

A VITAL PART of the good life in Christ is the particular church or assembly of Christians with whom you choose to fellowship. You will pray with them, learn more of God's word with them and serve with them.

It is true that we can fellowship with our heavenly Father alone, we can pray alone, we can study God's word alone and we can serve God alone – all of which we should do and will do, if we have truly received Christ into our lives.

But it is a fact that we prove our love for God best when we express His love toward others. *If you love not your brother or sister whom you have seen, how can you love God whom you have not seen? And this commandment have we from him, that to love God you love others also.*[1Jn.4:20-21]

It is also a fact that we serve God best when we serve others. *God is love* [1Jn.4:8, 16] and *love is of God.*[1Jn.4:7] *Every one that loves is born of God, and knows God.*[1Jn.4:7] *If God loved us, we ought to lay down our lives for others.*[1Jn.4:11; 1Jn.3:16]

A new commandment I give you, that you love one

another; as I have loved you, that you also love one another. By this shall everyone know that you are my disciples, if you love one another.[Jn.13:34-35]

It is scriptural that we worship God with a company of believers; that we pray in His sanctuary; that we be taught in the ways of God and of His word by a shepherd — a pastor.

Paul says, *There is one body, and one Spirit, even as you are called in one hope of your calling; One Lord, one faith, one baptism, one God and Father of all, who is above all, and through all, and in you all.*

But to everyone of us is given grace according to the measure of the gift of Christ.[Ep.4:4-7]

He gave gifts to people. He gave some, apostles; and some, prophets; and some, evangelists; and some, pastors and teachers;

For the perfecting of the saints, for the work of the ministry, for the edifying of the body of Christ:

Till we all come in the unity of the faith, and of the knowledge of the Son of God, to perfection, to the measure of the stature of the fulness of Christ.[Ep.4:8, 11-13]

The great problem is that young Christians become confused by different denominations and church groups which sometimes contradict each other and seek to proselyte members.

This problem is caused by theologians who seem to feel that you cannot accept the Bible literally, but that it must have careful, technical interpretation. These religious agents believe that their school of training is the only true one. Often, as Jesus said, they *strain at a gnat, and swallow a camel.*[Mt.23:24]

We need not be confused by this multiplicity of doctrines and interpretations. We are not critical of those who earnestly condemn others while praising their own doctrinal stand. Paul gives some worthy counsel in this regard in the twelfth chapter of Romans.[Ro.12:6-10]

Remember that if true Christianity was as complex as some theologians make it seem, average folks could never be saved — non-Christians in other lands could never be converted.

Keep your eyes on Jesus Christ and on what He said.[He.12:2-3] Follow Him. His life is simple.[1Pe.2:21-23] His words can be understood by the most ordinary person. You cannot lose your way if you follow Him.[Jn.8:12; Jn.10:27-29]

Across the world, for nearly 40 years, we have been privileged to lead tens of thousands of non-Christians to accept Christ and to be born again. Then we have helped them find a company of believers — a good church, and to be faithful in worshiping, praying, studying, and fellowshiping together with them. But I am always concerned, because I have observed that when they seek for that fellowship, they are going to discover divisions which may precipitate confusion in their tender new faith.

My strongest counsel is to follow Jesus Christ.[Mt.16:24-27; Jn.1:43; Jn.12:26; Jn.21:19-22]

Be kind and understanding toward other believers.[1Co.13:4; Ep.4:30-32]

If they accuse and condemn Christians of other churches, do not absorb their bitterness.[He.12:14-15; Ph.4:7-8] Keep your own heart pure and judge no one.[Mt.7:1-5; Ro.14:12-13; Co.3:12-15] Love everyone and be an influence for understanding and good.[Ep.5:12; Ga.6:1-3; Ro.12:9-10; 1Th.3:12-13]

Keep this basic rule in mind: There can be only one true church — the body of Christ.[1Co.12:27; 1Co.3:11; Ep.4:4-6] It is made up of real Christians — of all who believe in Christ and His gospel.

An authentic Christian is one who:

Believes that Jesus Christ is God's Son;[Mt.16:16; Jn.1:49; Jn.3:35-36] conceived of the Holy Ghost;[Lu.1:34-35] born of a virgin;[Is.7:14; Mt.1:23] who came as God in the flesh;[Jn.1:14; Jn.14:6-11; Ro.8:3] who bore our sins for us in His death on the cross;[1Pe.2:24] who shed His blood for the remission of our sins;[Mt.26:28; Ep.1:7] who died for us and was raised from the dead for our justification;[1Co.15:4; Ro.4:25] who is now seated at God's right hand;[Ep.1:20; He.10:12; He.12:2; Co.3:1] who forever makes intercession for us.[He.7:25; 1Ti.2:5]

All who believe those facts of the gospel and who have come to God in faith, confessing their sins, and who have repented and called on the name of Jesus, accepting Him by faith, and who have confessed Christ as Savior before others and who believe on Him as their personal Savior, they are born into the one true church of Jesus Christ and are children of God, regardless of what company of Christians they fellowship and worship and sing and pray and study with.

Following Christ means to love, to serve, to worship, to learn, to fellowship. All of this can best be expressed through your social relationships developed in a local community of Christian believers.

The Bible says, *Forsake not the assembling of yourselves together, as the manner of some is.*[He.10:25]

I recommend that you do your best to find a company of Christians who believe in the fundamentals of the gospel mentioned above. Then be faithful as a member among them. Cooperate with your pastor. God has appointed him to be shepherd of the flock.[Je.3:15; Je.23:4]

God's word charges him: *Take heed therefore to yourself, and to the flock, over which the Holy Ghost has made you overseer, to feed the church of God, which he has purchased with his own blood.*[Ac.20:28]

Respect the pastor [1Pe.5:2; He.13:17] and seek to assist him in every plan to further the cause of Christ in your community — and abroad.

In case you cannot locate an already established church (or community of believers) in your area where you can attend regularly and be edified in your faith, and where you can have fellowship in worship and Christian service, then do what the early Christians had to do: They made their house a place of prayer and Bible study, and welcomed others to worship, study and pray with them.[Ac.2:46-47; Ac.5:42; Ac.12:12; Ac.20:20; Ac.28:30-31]

In fact, this was the way New Testament churches began,[Ro.16:5; 1Co.16:19; Co.4:15; Phm.2] so it would certainly be scriptural for your community, if necessary.

Jesus made a profound statement about the founding of His church. The true church is founded upon the revelation of faith that Jesus Christ is the Son of God. In other words, if you really believe that fact, if God has caused it to be revealed to your heart that Jesus was truly conceived of the Holy Ghost and born of a virgin and therefore of divine blood and the Son of God — actually God in the flesh — and if you have confessed that, then you are part of His true church because that revelation is the very foundation of the church.

He asked: *Whom do people say that I am?*[Mt.16:13]

They gave different answers, but Peter said, *You are the Christ, the Son of the living God.*[Mt.16:16]

Jesus responded: *Blessed are you, for flesh and*

blood has not revealed it to you, but my Father which is in heaven and on this rock I will build my church; and the gates of hell shall not prevail against it.[Mt.16:17-18]

If you believe those facts, you are part of Christ's church — His body, and all of hell cannot destroy your position nor put you out of His church.

Membership in local Christian communities is only symbolic. Human beings such as local pastors, teachers and fellow members may assist you and teach you, or they may judge you, admit you or exclude you.

But what counts is: Are you born again? Do you believe in Jesus Christ? Has He received you into the one church by your new birth? You see, you may join any church but you must be reborn by a spiritual miracle to become a member of the true church of Jesus Christ.

There are three facts about the one true church — the body of Christ — the community of all true believers throughout the world:

1. Jesus Christ Himself founded it.

On this rock (of revelation by faith that I am the Son of God) *will I build my church.*[Mt.16:17-18]

2. Jesus is the cornerstone.

Now you are fellow citizens with the saints, and of the household of God: and are built upon the founda-

tion of the apostles and prophets, Jesus Christ himself being the chief corner stone.[Ep.2:19-20]

3. Jesus is the foundation.

Other foundation can no one lay than that is laid, which is Jesus Christ.[1Co.3:11]

Christ is the founder, the builder, and the church belongs to Him alone.

Christ loved the church, and gave himself for it: that he might sanctify and cleanse it with the washing of water by the word, that he might present it to himself a glorious church, not having spot, or wrinkle, or any such thing; but that it should be holy and without blemish.[Ep.5:25-27]

For we are members of his body, of his flesh, and of his bones. This is a great mystery: but I speak concerning Christ and the church.[Ep.5:30, 32]

The apostle Paul said that the essence of the true church is *Christ in you, the hope of glory.*[Co.1:27]

You are the temple of the living God; as God has said, I will dwell in them, and walk in them; and I shall be their God, and they shall be my people.[2Co.6:16]

There is just one church. You may join and fellowship with a community of believers in your area, but your real membership, your new spiritual birth and birthright is registered in the *Lamb's book of life in heaven.*[Re.21:27]

Like the telephone or railroad or postal systems,

there is one commanding head from which comes all basic orders. Those orders are executed and interpreted by many subordinate authorities, but there is only one head, and that is Christ.

That is why we follow Christ. We study His life. We learn His words. We live like He lived. We think like He thought. We talk like He talked. We act like He acted.

Express His love and mercy and compassion and understanding and you will know the joy and peace and fulfillment of true Christian living. Only that way can you really live the good life.

The underlying, basic beliefs and doctrines of all Christian denominations are fundamentally the same:

1. Jesus Christ was conceived of the Holy Ghost.[Mt.1:20; Lu.1:31, 35]

2. He was born of a virgin.[Mt.1:23; Lu.1:26-28]

3. He was God in the flesh, Emmanuel, God with us.[Is.7:14; Mt.1:23]

4. His blood was Divine.[Mt.26:28; Ro.5:9; Ep.1:7; Ep.2:13; Co.1:14, 20; He.10:19; He.13:20-21; 1Pe.1:18-19; 1Jn.1:7; Re.1:5]

5. His life showed us the will of God.[Jn.6:38; He.10:7, 9]

6. He died to pay our debt, bearing our sins.[Jn.3:16-17; Ro.6:6-8; 1Co.15:3; 2Co.5:21; 1Th.5:9-10; 1Pe.2:24]

7. He rose again for our justification.[Ro.3:24-25;

Ro.4:25; Ro.5:1

8. He lives today seated at God's right hand to continually make intercession for us as the only mediator between us and God.*Ro.8:34; Ep.1:20; Co.3:1; 1Ti.2:5; He.1:3; He.7:25; He.8:1, 6; He.9:15; He.10:12; He.12:2, 24; 1Pe.3:22; Re.1:18*

9. He is the only Savior.*Mt.1:21; Lu.2:11; Lu.24:46-47; Jn.4:42; Jn.14:6; Ac.4:12; Ac.5:31; Ph.3:20; 2Ti.1:10; Ti.3:6; 2Pe.1:11; 1Jn.4:14*

All Christian churches agree on these fundamentals, but unfortunately there is always denominational conflict about the peripheral and non-essential doctrines, ceremonies, rituals and forms of expressing and propagating Christianity.

Amidst this conflict, remember that you were called by Jesus Christ, and your principal responsibility is to follow Him and His word.*Jn.5:24*

Jesus said, *I am the light of the world: when you follow me you shall not walk in darkness.Jn.8:12*

When Jesus founded His church, He intended that all who believe in Him should unite in one common love and bond to serve Him together by serving others; to love and reach out together, as His body, to express His love and light and lift to the world; *until finally we all believe alike about our salvation and about our Savior, God's Son, and all become full-grown in the Lord – yes, to the point of being filled full with Christ. Then we will no longer be like children, forever changing our minds about what we believe because someone has told us something different. Instead, we will lovingly follow truth at all times – speaking truly, dealing truly, living truly – and so become more and more in every way like Christ who is the Head of his body, the church.* Ep.4:13-16 LB

The local community of believers whom you choose to assemble, to pray, to worship and to serve with will be of inestimable blessing and influence upon you and your household.

Your children will be taught in the ways of Christ.

The company of fellow believers will be witnesses at Christian marriages in your family.

They will unite in prayer and faith with you when you are sick or suffering trials or crises.

They will support you and comfort you in times of bereavement.

They will be your fellow believers.

They will encourage and strengthen you.

They will pray with and for you

They will share truth with you.

They will worship with you.

They will love you

They will offer you the greatest opportunity to express your own faith and love by serving and helping others in an organized way with them.

The fellowship you will enjoy is really a foretaste of heaven because you will spend eternity with those who are true to their faith. Since you love people and love to fellowship with them and serve and worship with them, you are experiencing a bit of heaven right here on earth.

In essence, the church of Jesus Christ – His body – constitutes the only feet and eyes and ears and arms Christ has here on earth. You are His body so let Him love through you. Let Him see human needs through your eyes. Let Him care about those needs through your heart of love. Let Him express that love through your life. Let Him prove that love through your hands and feet and arms and all that you are and do.

The Church is you.

You are Christ's body. He lives in you and expresses Himself and His love through you.

That, in essence, is the good life.

Chapter 28

Standards for the Good Life

TO REALIZE THE BENEFITS of the good life with Christ, our faith in Him must rest entirely on the word of God.

That is why you will want to read the Bible daily and let it be the standard for your life.

You may think that you cannot understand the Bible but Jesus said: *I thank you, O Father, Lord of heaven and earth, because you have hid these things from the wise and prudent, and have revealed them to babes. Even so, Father: for it seemed good in your sight.*[Mt.11:25-26]

The Bible is the simplest book of all to understand. It is called a revelation. When something is revealed, it is clear. The Holy Spirit will open your understanding so you can comprehend it, if you will just read it.[Jn.14:26; 1Jn.2:27]

Blessed are they that read, and they that hear the words of this prophecy.[Re.1:3]

Another reason you can understand it is because every truth is repeated over and over. *In the mouth of two or three witnesses shall every word be es-*

tablished.[De.17:6; De.19:15; Mt.18:16; 2Co.13:1; 1Ti.5:19; He.10:28] That principle is mentioned repeatedly in the Bible. If something is not repeated enough to be absolutely clear, it is not a vital doctrine which is essential to your salvation.

The Bible is simple because it is written in clear language and it needs no interpretation. The Bible is a book to be accepted exactly as it is written. It means what it says.

God is the author, so He needs no assistance. He is the master-communicator. He has said what He means. Accept it. People who say the Bible is difficult to understand usually do not want to believe what it says.

Remember that it was written to be understood by the most unlearned and simple people, so that even the *wayfaring, though fools, shall not err therein.*[Is.35:8]

Paul said to Timothy, *From a child you have known the holy scriptures.*[2Ti.3:15] He speaks of *the simplicity that is in Christ.*[2Co.11:3]

The learned religious leaders in Jerusalem who arrested Peter and John because of the miraculous healing of a crippled man were dumbfounded by this undeniable wonder.[Ac.3:1-9] Certainly no credit could go to these two men: *When they saw Peter and John, they perceived that they were unlearned and ignorant men*[Ac.4:13]

Another reason the Bible is easy enough to understand is that God expects people to hear it and to believe it to be saved. Since salvation is for *whoever will,* the Bible must be simple enough for anyone to understand. *Whoever believes* (the gospel) *shall not perish, but have everlasting life.*[Jn.3:16]

Abraham Lincoln said, "Take all of the Bible that you can by reason and the balance by faith, and you will live and die a better person. It is the best book which God has given to humankind."

Napoleon Bonaparte said, "The Bible is more than a book; it is a living being with an action, a power which invades everything that opposes its extension."

Woodrow Wilson said, "A person has deprived themself of the best there is in the world who has deprived themself of the Bible."

Eight hundred scientists of Great Britain signed a statement recorded in the Bodelian Library at Oxford, which, among other things, declared: "We conceive that it is impossible for the word of God written in the book of nature, and God's word written in holy scripture, to contradict one another." Their objective was to "express sincere regret that researchers into scientific truth are perverted ... into ... casting doubt upon the truth and authenticity of the holy scripture."

Daniel Webster, 19th Century American statesman, said, "The Bible is the book of faith, and a book of doctrine, and a book of morals, and a book of religion, of special revelation from God; but it is a book which teaches human beings their responsibility, their own dignity, and their equality with their fellow human beings."

Those who wrote the Bible claim to have been inspired of God. They indeed were, or they were liars. It is hard to conceive that over forty different authors would have the same idea to lie about the same thing. Those forty people wrote sixty-six books during more than 1600 years about one central theme of creation and redemption by God through Jesus Christ and the Holy Spirit, and were not in contact with each other (except the apostles).

It really does not make sense that, being spread across nearly 20 centuries of varying societies, they would all conceive a common deception.

Nor does it make sense to doubt the Bible because the creation story or the resurrection of Christ cannot be scientifically verified. Critics ridicule Christian believers by asking: "Were you there when God supposedly created the world?" or "Were you there when Jesus Christ was said to have raised from the dead?" But the same questions apply to unbelievers. They were not there when spinning evolution of the universe was supposed to have taken place. Were they there when lower forms of life evolved from their surrounding mass of confusion and followed their mysterious interrelated phenomena of development to the status of humankind?

If evolution was the correct theory, it would seem that when you die, you would return, by reverse process, to the confusion from where you are alleged to have evolved.

But you do not. You return to the dust. Every grave on earth bears scientific proof of this fact. Given enough time, only dust remains And dust is the substance out of which the Bible says God first created Adam:

And the Lord God formed man of the dust of the ground, and breathed into his nostrils the breath of life; and man became a living soul.[Ge.2:7]

And every human being that dies returns to dust.

All of the basic questions of our origin, our existence, our purpose and our destiny are clearly answered in the Bible, by forty different authors who wrote 66 books spanning over 1,600 years. If they all lied about their being led of God to write, it seems extremely illogical to believe that so many great and honorable people of their times would conceive the same deception.

It makes sense to me to believe the Bible and to trust God's written promises.[Jn.5:24]

The Bible was written on two continents, in

countries separated by hundreds of miles, spanning over sixteen centuries of time. Part of it was written in Syria, another portion in Arabia. Part of it was written in Italy and Greece. Some of it was written in the desert of Sinai, some in the wilderness of Judea. Part was penned in the cave of Adullam, some in the prison of Rome. Some came from the Isle of Patmos and other parts from the palaces of Mt. Zion and Shushan. Some portions were written by the rivers of Babylon and some on the banks of the Chebar.

There exists no literary phenomenon in the world to compare with the Bible. It was written by herdsmen, shepherds, fishermen, politicians, princes, poets, philosophers, statesmen, prophets, priests, publicans and physicians.

Every form of literary structure is displayed. There is history, poetry, prose, prophecy, letters, proverbs, parables, allegories and orations.

Yet there is no discord. Its unity and cohesion are one of the great miracles of human history. There is perfect harmony from Genesis to Revelation. Everything in it agrees with all the rest of it, because it was inspired by one master-designer — God. It constitutes one unit, each section being interwoven in the other sections although the authors lived in epochs spanning nearly two millenniums.

Can you imagine the incoherent labyrinth that

would result in one volume like the Bible if forty clerks, judges, politicians, rulers, fishermen, clergymen, doctors, laborers and other types of people, spanning sixteen centuries, had written on almost any subject? It could only be a disorganized, and inharmonious.

Take the subject of medical science alone. Can you imagine the contradiction of information that would be evidenced by writers spanning so many centuries.

Yet the Bible, which treats subjects covering the whole range of human inquiry, is one book, without a flaw of incoherency, containing one system of doctrine, one plan of salvation, one order of ethics, one rule of faith, one story of love and redemption from one curse of sin.

The Bible *came not in old time by the will of man: but holy men of God spoke* (and wrote) *as they were moved by the Holy Ghost.*[2Pe.1:21] That is the secret of this literary miracle which we call the Bible, and that is why all parts of it are so intertwined with the others.

The Ten Commandments which were given to Moses find their only fulfillment in Christ's Sermon on the Mount, recorded 1,500 years later.

Isaiah's prophecies, written 700 years before Christ, are unfolded in the record of the gospels.

The book of Daniel, written about events dating

from 605 to 535 B.C., and the Revelation, written in the year 96 A.D., fit together in perfect precision.

Leviticus, dating 1491 B.C., defines the epistle to the Hebrews written 1555 years later in 64 A.D. Then Hebrews, in turn, is only understood by comparing it with the book of Leviticus.

The last book of the Bible is like a dome flashing in noonday splendor to crown its whole unity and is mysteriously entwined with the very first chapters of the Bible.

The story of Christ is gradually unveiled throughout the Bible: 1) In the Old Testament, the preparation for the coming of Christ is made; 2) the four gospels are the record of His manifestation; 3) the book of Acts records the propagation of Christ's gospel; 4) the epistles contain the explanation of His message; 5) in the Revelation we have presented the consummation of His return.

The great American evangelist, Billy Sunday, wrote a most marvelous and eloquent tribute to the Bible:

"With the Holy Spirit as my guide, I entered at the portico of Genesis, walked down the corridor of the Old Testament art-galleries, where pictures of Noah, Abraham, Moses, Joseph, Isaac, Jacob, and Daniel hang on the wall. I passed into the music room of the Psalms where the Spirit sweeps the keyboard of nature until it seems that every reed and pipe in God's great organ responds to the harp of David, the sweet singer of Israel.

"I entered the chamber of Ecclesiastes, where the voice of the preacher is heard, and into the conservatory of Sharon and the lily of the valley where sweet spices filled and perfumed my life.

"I entered the business office of Proverbs and on into the observatory of the prophets where I saw telescopes of various sizes pointing to far off events, concentrating on the bright and morning Star which was to rise over the moonlit hills of Judea for our salvation and redemption.

"I entered the audience room of the King of kings, catching a vision written by Matthew, Mark, Luke, and John. Thence into the correspondence room with Paul, Peter, James and John writing their epistles.

"I stepped into the throne room of Revelation where tower the glittering peaks, where sits the King of kings upon His throne of glory with the healing of the nations in His hand, and I cried out:

All hail the power of Jesus' name, Let angels prostrate fall; Bring forth the royal diadem, And crown Him Lord of all.

Chapter 29

Tenets of the Christian Faith

I HAVE OUTLINED eighteen basic Christian fundamentals which will help you to grow with God in the good life. They are by no means comprehensive, but they will help to acquaint you with your Bible.

1. THE SCRIPTURES

THE HOLY BIBLE was written by human persons divinely inspired. It is a perfect treasure of heavenly instruction. God is its author. Salvation is its end. Truth, without error, is its essence. It reveals the principles by which God has saved us, and therefore is, and shall remain to the end of the world, the true basis for Christian living, and the supreme standard by which all human conduct, creeds, and opinions are to be measured.

All scripture is given by inspiration of God, and is profitable for doctrine, for reproof, for correction, for instruction in righteousness: That you may be perfect, thoroughly furnished to all good works. [2Ti.3:16-17; 2Pe.1:21; 2S.23:2; Ac.1:16; Ac.3:21; Jn.10:35; Lu.16:29-31; Ps.119:3; Ro.3:1-2]

Every word of God is pure: He is a shield to them that put their trust in him. [Pr.30:5; Jn.17:17; Re.22:18]

For as many as have sinned in the law shall be judged by the law.[Ro.2:12; Ro.3:4] *And if you hear my words, the word that I have spoken, the same shall judge you in the last day.*[Jn.12:47-48; 1Co.4:3-4; Lu.10:10-16; Lu.12:47-48]

2. THE TRUE GOD

THERE IS ONE living and true God, an infinite, all intelligent Spirit, whose name is Jehovah, the eternally self-existent, self-revealed *I AM*,[Is.44:6; Is.45:18] the creator and supreme ruler of heaven and earth, inexpressibly glorious in holiness, and worthy of all possible honor, confidence and love. In the unity of His being, the three persons of the Father, the Son, and the Holy Ghost are one in divine perfection, having united, though distinct offices in the great work of the redemption of humankind.

God is a Spirit.[Jn.4:24] *His understanding is infinite.*[Ps.147:5] *You whose name alone is Jehovah, are the most high over all the earth.*[Ps.83:18; He.3:4; Ro.1:20; Je.10:10]

Who is like you, glorious in holiness? [Ex.15:11; Is.6:3; 1Pe.1:15-16; Re.4:6-8]

And you shall love the Lord your God with all your heart, and with all your soul, and with all your mind, and with all your strength.[Mk.12:30]

You are worthy, O Lord, to receive glory, and honor, and power.[Re.4:11]

3. THE FALL OF HUMANKIND

THE SCRIPTURES teach that God created humankind *in His own image,*[Ge.1:27] to share His own life, love and purpose. They were of infinite value to Him. He asked only that they trust His word, but they chose to disbelieve it and that opened the way for deterioration and death. They were separated from God to become the slaves of Satan, and the seed of distrust was bred into all of their descendants.

So God created humankind in his own image.[Ge.1:27] *And God saw everything he had made, and behold it was very good.*[Ge.1:31]

And when the woman saw that the tree was good for food, she took the fruit and ate, and gave it to her husband with her; and he ate.[Ge.3:6-24; Ro.5:12]

By one person's disobedience many were made sinners.[Ro.5:19; Jn.3:6; Ps.51:5; Ro.5:15-19; Ro.8:7] *We have turned, every one to our own way.*[Is.53:6; Ge.6:12; Ro.3:9-18]

Among whom also we had our conversation in times past in the lusts of our flesh and of the mind; and were by nature the children of wrath, even as others.[Ep.2:3; Ro.1:18-32; Ro.2:1-16; Ga.3:10; Mt.20:15]

4. THE WAY OF SALVATION

THE SALVATION of people is by grace alone, through Jesus Christ, who assumed our nature, yet without sin; then, He endured the judgment of our sins when He died on the cross, and He justified us, restoring us to God as though we had never sinned. Being raised from the dead, He now lives as our Representative, Savior and Lord.

By grace you are saved.[Ep.2:5; Mt.18:11; 1Jn.4:10; 1Co.3:5-7; Ac.15:11]

For God so loved the world, that he gave his only begotten Son, that whoever believes in him should not perish, but have everlasting life.[Jn.3:16; Jn.1:1-4; He.4:14; He.12:24]

Who being in the form of God, thought it not robbery to be equal with God: but made himself of no reputation, and took upon him the form of a servant, and was made in the likeness of men.[Ph.2:6-7; He.2:9, 14; 2Co.5:21]

He was wounded for our transgressions, he was bruised for our iniquities: The chastisement of our peace was upon him; and with his stripes we are healed.[Is.53:4-5]

He is able also to save them to the uttermost that come to God by him, seeing he ever lives to make intercession for them.[He.7:25] *For in him dwells all the fulness of the godhead bodily.*[Co.2:9; He.2:8; He.7:26]

5. REGENERATION

REGENERATION, or the new birth, is the miracle experienced by those who believe that Jesus redeemed them. They receive the impartation of His life and righteousness, and experience a recreation, a re-birth, a transformation from sinfulness to righteousness, from deterioration to the nature and the life of God. Jesus Christ is accepted by faith and embraced as the source of their new life.

Verily, verily, I say to you, except you be born again, you cannot see the kingdom of God.[Jn.3:3]

That which is born of the flesh is flesh; and that which is born of the Spirit is spirit.[Jn.3:6]

Being born again, not of corruptible seed, but of incorruptible, by the word of God.[1Pe.1:23]

Of his own will he begat us with the word of truth.[Ja.1:18]

If any one be in Christ, they are a new creature.[2Co.5:17]

You know that every one that does righteousness is born of him.[1Jn.2:29]

And that you put on the new self, which after God is created in righteousness and true holiness.[Ep.4:24]

And you being dead in your sins, and the uncircumcision of your flesh, has he quickened together with him.[Co.2:13]

Yield yourselves to God, as those that are alive from the dead.[Ro.6:13]

Who has delivered us from the power of darkness, and has translated us into the kingdom of his dear Son.[Co.1:13]

Which were born, not of blood, nor of the will of the flesh, nor of the will of a human person, but of

God.[Jn.1:13]

And such were some of you: But you are washed, but you are sanctified, but you are justified, in the name of the Lord Jesus, and by the Spirit of our God.[1Co.6:11]

6. REPENTANCE

REPENTANCE IS A personal act, prompted by the Spirit of God, by which a change of mind and of will is effected in those who have heard that, because of Christ's divine love, He suffered the judgment of their sins in order to redeem them; and who therefore resolve to turn away from sins and to accept the righteousness of Jesus by faith.

In those days came John the Baptist, preaching in the wilderness of Judea, and saying, Repent, for the kingdom of heaven is at hand.[Mt.3:1-2]

From that time Jesus began to preach, and to say, Repent: For the kingdom of heaven is at hand.[Mt.4:17]

And saying, The time is fulfilled, and the kingdom of God is at hand: Repent and believe the gospel.[Mk.1:15]

Repent therefore, and be converted, that your sins may be blotted out.[Ac.3:19]

And the times of this ignorance God winked at; but now commands all people everywhere to repent.[Ac.17:30]

Testifying both to the Jews, and also to the Greeks, repentance toward God, and faith toward our Lord Jesus Christ.[Ac.20:21]

For godly sorrow works repentance to salvation not

to be repented of.[2Co.7:10]

And that repentance and remission of sins should be preached in his name among all nations, beginning at Jerusalem.[Lu.24:47]

Him has God exalted with his right hand to be a Prince and a Savior, for to give repentance to Israel, and forgiveness of sins.[Ac.5:31]

But after your hardness and impenitent heart you treasure up to yourself wrath against the day of wrath and revelation of the righteous judgment of God.[Ro.2:5]

Let the wicked forsake their way, and the unrighteous their thoughts: And let them return to the Lord, and he will have mercy; and to our God for he will abundantly pardon.[Is.55:7]

7. FAITH

FAITH IS ACCEPTING, without question, the fact that God's word is infallible and unequivocally trustworthy. It is an assent of the mind and a consent of the heart, by which the believer is brought into vital relation with God, freely justified, and lives fully trusting Christ for salvation, and it commits the heart and life to Him.

Believe on the Lord Jesus Christ, and you shall be saved.[Ac.16:31]

For Christ is the end of the law for righteousness to everyone that believes.[Ro.10:4]

Therefore being justified by faith, we have peace with

God through our Lord Jesus Christ.[Ro.5:1]

Now faith is the substance of things hoped for, the evidence of things not seen.[He.11:1]

But without faith it is impossible to please him.[He.11:6]

For therein is the righteousness of God revealed from faith to faith: As it is written, The just shall live by faith.[Ro.1:17]

And the scripture was fulfilled which says, Abraham believed God, and it was imputed to him for righteousness.[Ja.2:23]

Blessed is the one who trusts in the Lord, and whose hope the Lord is.[Je.17:7]

They that trust in the Lord shall be as Mount Zion, which cannot be removed but abides forever.[Ps.125:1]

The Lord redeems the soul of his servants: And none of them that trust in Him shall be desolate.[Ps.34:22]

For we walk by faith, not by sight.[2Co.5:7]

Even the righteousness of God which is by faith of Jesus Christ to all and on all them that believe.[Ro.3:22]

For with the heart you believe to righteousness; and with your mouth confession is made to salvation.[Ro.10:10]

8. JUSTIFICATION

JUSTIFICATION is the state of being restored to God, as His friend and partner, as though no sin had ever been committed, because Jesus Christ legally endured all of the judgment of our sins on the cross. He did it to prove how much God loves us. Since no penalty can be adjudged twice and no debt can be paid twice, we are no longer guilty. By God's infinite favor, we are regenerated and redeemed as though we had never sinned.

And of his fulness we have all received. Jn.1:16; Ep.3:8

And by him all that believe are justified from all things. Ac.13:39; Is.53:11-12; Ro.8:1

Being now justified by his blood, we shall be saved from wrath through him. Ro.5:9; Zec.13:1; Ac.10:43

Therefore being justified by faith, we have peace with God through our Lord Jesus Christ: By whom also we have access by faith into this grace wherein we stand, and rejoice in hope of the glory of God. Ro.5:1-2; Ro.6:11; 1Co.1:30-31; 1Ti.4:8

9. THE BODY OF CHRIST

THE CHURCH IS THE body of Christ, consisting of all who accept Jesus Christ as their only Savior from sin, who trust the merits of His sacrifice and of His blood as the only remission of their sins, and who confess Him as Lord and master of their own lives. The body of Christ is collectively all believers, and individually each believer. The real church is the real Christian. Christ lives in the believer and He expresses His ministry of compassion, His love, His life, and His words through the Christian believer, who is His church, His body.

Now you are the body of Christ, and members in particular.[1Co.12:27; Ro.12:4-5; Ep.1:20-23; Co.1:18-24]

What? Know you not that your body is the temple of the Holy Ghost which is in you, which you have of God, and you are not your own?[1Co.6:19; Ph.1:20-21]

And what agreement has the temple of God with idols? For you are the temple of the living God; as God has said, I will dwell in them, and walk in them; and I will be their God, and they shall be my people.[2Co.6:16; He.3:6]

In whom all the building fitly framed together grows to a holy temple in the Lord: In whom you also are builded together for an habitation of God through the Spirit.[Ep.2:21-22]

For we are members of his body, of his flesh, and of his bones.[Ep.5:30; 1Co.12:12-20; Ep.4:15-16; Ph.1:20-21]

10. CHRISTIAN BAPTISM

THOSE WHO BELIEVE in and confess Jesus Christ as their personal Savior follow His example by being baptized in water.

It is an outward sign of an inward work, a public testimony that symbolizes the fact that, as Christ died on the cross, so we reckon ourselves now dead to sin.

As Christ was buried, so we are buried with Him by baptism.

As Christ was raised from the dead, so we are raised from the water with His new life in us.

Therefore we are buried with him by baptism into death: That like as Christ was raised up from the dead by the glory of the Father, even so we also should walk in newness of life.[Ro.6:4; Ac.10:48; Ac.22:16; Co.2:12; 1Pe.3:20-21]

And the eunuch said, See here is water; what hinders me to be baptized? And Philip said, If you believe with all your heart, you may and they went down both into the water, both Philip and the eunuch; and he baptized him.[Ac.8:36-38; Mt.3:5-6; Mt.28:19; Mk.16:16; Jn.3:22-23; Ac.2:38; Ac.8:12; Ac.16:32-34; Ac.18:8]

Go, and teach all nations, baptizing them in the name of the Father, and of the Holy Ghost.[Mt.28:19; Ac.10:47-48]

Repent, and be baptized every one of you in the name of Jesus Christ for the remission of sins, and you shall receive the gift of the Holy Ghost.[Ac.2:38]

Can any one forbid water, that these should not be baptized and he commanded them to be baptized in the name of the Lord.[Ac.10:47-48; Ga.3:27-28]

Then they that gladly received his word were baptized, and there were added to them, the same day, about three thousand souls. And they continued steadfastly in the apostles' doctrine and fellowship, and in breaking of bread, and in prayers.[Ac.2:41-42]

11. THE LORD'S SUPPER

THE LORD'S SUPPER consists of bread and

wine, as symbols of Christ's body and blood, partaken of by Christian believers, in memory of the sacrifice of our Lord Jesus Christ. By these emblems, Christians show their faith in Christ's love, and in eternal life through His resurrection.

And he took bread, and gave thanks, and broke it, and gave it to them, saying, This is my body which is given for you: This do in remembrance of me. Likewise also the cup after supper saying, This cup is the new testament in my blood, which is shed for you.[Lu.22:19-20; Mk.14:20-26; Mt.26:26-30; 1Co.10:16; 1Co.11:27-30]

For as often as you eat this bread, and drink this cup, you do show the Lord's death till he comes.[1Co.11:26; Mt.28:20]

But examine yourself, and so eat of that bread, and drink of that cup.[1Co.11:28; Ac.2:42-46; Ac.20:7-11]

And they continued steadfastly in the apostles' doctrine and fellowship and in breaking of bread and in prayers.[Ac.2:42]

12. SPIRITUAL AND PHYSICAL HEALING

GOD CREATED HUMANKIND in perfect harmony with himself. It is His will for our spirit, soul and body to be strong. In the Old Testament, God's covenant includes healing for our physical sicknesses and diseases. This covenant was ratified by Christ's ministry of healing in the gospels. The apostolic church taught and practiced divine healing for the physical body. The ministry of the church, as instituted by Christ and confirmed by the Holy Spirit through the apostolic church remains unchanged today.

As many (sinners) *as received him were born of God.*[Jn.1:12-13] *As many* (sick) *as touched him were made whole.*[Mk.6:56]

If you will diligently hearken to the voice of the Lord your God, and will do that which is right in his sight, I will put none of these diseases on you for I am the Lord that heals you.[Ex.15:26]

Who forgives all your iniquities; who heals all your diseases.[Ps.103:3]

He was wounded for our transgressions, he was bruised for our iniquities: The chastisement of our peace was upon him; and with his stripes we are healed.[Is.53:5]

He (Christ) *healed all that were sick: That it might be fulfilled which was spoken by Esaias the prophet, saying, himself took our infirmities, and bore our sicknesses.*[Mt.8:16-17]

Who his own self bore our sins in his own body on the tree, that we, being dead to sins, should live to righteousness; by whose stripes you were healed.[1Pe.2:24]

I wish above all things that you may prosper and be in health, even as your soul prospers.[3Jn.2]

Jesus Christ the same yesterday, and to day, and for ever.[He.13:8]

If you are sick, call for the elders of the church; and let them pray over you, anointing you with oil in the name of the Lord. And the prayer of faith shall save you, and the Lord shall raise you up; and if you have committed sins, they shall be forgiven you.[Ja.5:14-15]

13. EVANGELISM AND THE HOLY SPIRIT

THE MISSION of Jesus Christ to the world is the redemption of humankind. He commissioned all believers to announce to all creatures the good news that He died for their sins, that He was raised for their justification and that He lives as their only Savior and Lord.

To accomplish this mission, Jesus told His followers to be endued with the power of the Holy Ghost which would enable them to give miracle proof that He is alive again, providing evidence to the world that the gospel message is true.

Christ Jesus came into the world to save sinners.[1Ti.1:15; Is.53:4-5; 1Co.15:3; Ti.2:14; Ga.3:13; He.2:9; 1Pe.2:24; 1Pe.3:18; 1Jn.3:5]

For the Son of man is come to seek and to save that which was lost.[Lu.19:10; Jn.3:17; Ac.5:31; He.7:25; 1Pe.1:18-20]

And all things are of God, who has reconciled us to himself by Jesus Christ, and has given to us the ministry of reconciliation.[2Co.5:18; Ep.2:16; Co.1:20; He.2:17]

Jesus said, Verily, I say to you, the Son can do nothing of himself.[Jn.5:19-20; Jn.15:5]

God anointed Jesus of Nazareth with the Holy Ghost

and with power. Ac.10:38; Lu.4:18; Lu.24:48-49

You shall receive power after that the Holy Ghost is come upon you: and you shall be witnesses unto me ... unto the uttermost part of the earth. Ac.1:8; Ac.2:32; Ac.3:15; Ac.4:33; Ac.5:32; Mt.24:14

Follow me, and I will make you fishers of people. Mt.4:19; Mt.28:19-20; Mk.16:15

14. GIVING AND RECEIVING

THE PRIMARY RESPONSIBILITY, and privilege, of all Christians is to give the gospel to *every creature* in *all the world.* Because this ministry is foremost in the church, all Christians are called by the scriptures to contribute financially of their material means for the ministry of evangelism.

Inasmuch as God created the wealth of this planet for the use and prosperity of His children who do His will, the financial support for all ministries of His church is to be provided by Christians who: (a) honor the Lord with their firstfruits; (b) who bring their tithes into the storehouse, and; (c) who give of their gifts for the soulwinning ministries of evangelism.

In so doing, God wills that they prosper financially, and be in health, even as their souls prosper. God wills that they increase in material possessions, according to His law of sowing and reaping, in the same way that a farmer reaps more than is sown, in order to have more to sow and thus more to reap.

The silver is mine, and the gold is mine, says the Lord.[Hag.2:8; Ex.19:5; Le.25:23; Ps.50:10]

Honor the Lord with your substance, and with the firstfruits of all your increase: So shall your barns be filled with plenty.[Pr.3:9-10]

Bring all the tithes into the storehouse and prove me now herewith, says the Lord of hosts, if I will not open you the windows of heaven, and pour you out a blessing, that there shall not be room enough to receive it.[Mal.3:10]

Give and it shall be given to you; good measure, pressed down, and shaken together, and running over, shall people give into your bosom. For with the same measure that you shall meet with. It shall be measured to you again.[Lu.6:38; 2Co.9:8; 1Ti.6:17-19]

The blessing of the Lord, it makes rich, and he adds no sorrow with it.[Pr.10:22; Ec.5:19; Ps.112:1-3]

If you sow sparingly, you shall reap also sparingly; and if you sow bountifully, you shall reap also bountifully.[2Co.9:6; Ga.6:7; Ac.20:35]

15. CIVIL GOVERNMENT

CIVIL GOVERNMENT IS OF divine appointment, for the interest and good order of human society. Officials are to be prayed for, conscientiously honored and obeyed, except in things opposed to the will of our Lord Jesus Christ, who is the only Lord of the conscience, and the Prince of the kings of the earth.

The powers that be are ordained of god, for rulers are not a terror to good works, but to the evil.[Ro.13:1-7]

Submit yourselves to every ordinance of law, for the Lord's sake.[1Pe.2:13]

Render to Caesar the things that are Caesar's, and to God the things that are God's.[Mt.22:21; Ti.3:1; 1Pe.2:13; 1Ti.2:1-8]

We ought to obey God rather than people.[Ac.5:29] *And fear not them which kill the body, but are not able to kill the soul.*[Mt.10:28; Da.3:15-18; Da.6:7-10; Ac.4:18-20]

For one is your master, even Christ.[Mt.23:10] *Who are you that judges another's servant?* [Ro.14:4] *And he has on his vesture and on his thigh a name written, King of kings and Lord of lords.*[Re.19:16; Ps.72:11; Ro.14:9-11]

16. THE WORLD TO COME

THE END OF THE WORLD is approaching. At the Last Day, a final separation will take place. Unbelievers will be sentenced to endless sorrow, and the righteous to endless joy and eternal perfection.

The end of the world is coming soon: Therefore, be earnest, thoughtful men and women of prayer.[1Pe.4:7 LB; 1Co.7:29-31; He.1:10-12; Mt.24:35; Mt.28:20; 1Jn.2:17]

This same Jesus, which is taken up from you into heaven, shall so come in like manner as you have seen him go into heaven.[Ac.1:11; Re.1:7; He.9:28; Ac.3:21]

There shall be a resurrection of the dead, both of the

just and unjust.[Ac.24:15; 1Co.15:12-58; Lu.14:14; Da.12:2; Jn.5:28-29; Jn.6:40; Jn.11:25-26; 2Ti.1:10; Ac.10:42] *The angels shall come forth, and sever the wicked from among the just.*[Mt.13:49; Mt.13:37-43; Mt.24:30-31]

And these shall go away into everlasting punishment, but the righteous to life eternal.[Mt.25:46]

Seeing then that all these things shall be dissolved, what manner of person ought you to be in all holy conversation and godliness, looking for and hastening to the coming of the day of God.[2Pe.3:11-12]

17. PERSONAL COMMITMENT

HAVING RECEIVED the Lord Jesus Christ, and having given myself wholly to Him, I do now resolve to walk in Him, with love toward others for His glory. Therefore, in His strength, I purpose:

That I will demonstrate genuine concern for others and will take every opportunity to lift and encourage all whom I meet;

That I will enjoy the fellowship of other believers, and will publicly acknowledge Jesus as my Savior and Lord;

That I will treasure family worship and teaching at home, and be faithful in scripturally training my children, and those under my influence to show their love for Christ by sharing His life and love with others;

That as I am the light of the world and the salt of the earth, I will practice the awareness of Jesus

Christ who is at work in and through me, and allow Him to use my eyes, my hands, my feet, and all that I am to express His life to others;

That I will systematically invest of my substance in the Lord's work, by bringing my first-fruits, my tithes, and my gifts for evangelism, so that God may prosper me for the expansion of His kingdom as I express and propagate the gospel to all people in all the world;

That I will in all conditions, even until death, strive to live to the glory of Him who has called me out of darkness into His marvelous light.

18. APOSTLES' CREED

THE MOST CONCISE form of the broad trans-fundamental Christian doctrine is set forth in the historic and revered Apostles' Creed, which has survived since the fourth century, and is regarded as the oldest summary of enduring Christian doctrine in existence. It was pronounced by Augustine as *brevis and grandis* — brief as to the number of words, grand as to the weight of its teachings. It expresses, in disencumbered clarity, the fundamental essentials of the Christian faith in general, which are as follows:

I believe in God the Father Almighty, Maker of heaven and earth;

I believe in Jesus Christ, His only Son, our Lord,

Who was conceived by the Holy Ghost,

Born of the virgin Mary,

Suffered under Pontius Pilate,

Was crucified, dead and buried.

He descended into hades.

The third day He rose again from the dead.

He ascended into heaven, and sits on the right hand of God Almighty;

From there He shall come to judge the quick and the dead.

I believe in the Holy Ghost; the one universal and apostolic Church; the communion of saints; the forgiveness of sins; the resurrection of the body; and the life everlasting. Amen.

Benediction

Now the God of peace, that brought again from the dead our Lord Jesus, that great Shepherd of the sheep, through the blood of the everlasting covenant, make you perfect in every good work to do his will, working in you that which is well pleasing in his sight through Jesus Christ, to whom be glory forever and ever. Amen. [He.13:20-21]

PART VIII

THE GOOD LIFE FOR YOU

WHAT GOD HAS DONE for others, it is His will to do for you.

The good life is for every man, woman, boy and girl who wants to fulfill God's dream for his or her life.

When you discover your roots in God and the abundance that He created for you, you begin to see your own real value and why He wills success, happiness, health and prosperity for you.

Here is the way to receive His best for your life spiritually, physically and materially. ➠

Chapter 30

How to be Saved

DID YOU EVER THROW a rope to a drowning person and have him or her clutch it while you pulled him or her to safety?

Did you ever rescue someone from a burning building? Did you ever save anyone? Did anyone ever save you?

I want to tell you how you can be saved from your sins, saved from death, saved from disease, saved from evil.

You can be saved right now.

The Bible says: *This is a faithful saying, and worthy of all acceptation, that Christ Jesus came into the world to save sinners.*[1Ti.1:15]

The angel said: *You shall call his name Jesus: for he shall save his people from their sins.*[Mt.1:21]

The Bible says: *God sent not his Son into the world to condemn the world; but that the world through him might be saved.*[Jn.3:17] And Peter said, *Whoever shall call on the name of the Lord shall be saved.*[Ac.2:21]

You were not made for a life of sin and disease. You were made to walk with God. But sin has separated you from God.[Is.59:2]

But now, thank God, Christ Jesus has *come into the world to save sinners.*[1Ti.1:15] He has come to save you.

What does it mean to be saved?

FIRST: It means to be born again — to become a child of God.

The Bible says: *As many as received him, to them gave he power to become the children of God.*[Jn.1:12]

What a marvel that you can receive a new birth and be born into God's royal family. You have been born once — born in sin — a child of sin — a servant of the devil. Now Christ says: *You must be born again.*[Jn.3:7] You must be converted — be saved — be changed — be made new.

If you will receive Christ Jesus into your life today, you will become a child of God, for *Christ came to save sinners.*[1Ti.1:15] Do you want to be born again today?

What else does it mean to be saved?

SECOND: It means to receive a new spiritual life.

Paul says: *If anyone be in Christ, that one is a new creature and all things are become new.*[2Co.5:17]

That is exactly what happens when Christ saves you. A conversion takes place. Old desires, habits and diseases pass away. All things become new.

You receive Christ's new life.

He said: *I am come that they might have life, and that they might have it more abundantly.*[Jn.10:10]

Do you want to receive His new life now?

THIRD: It means to receive peace.

Jesus said: *Peace I leave with you, my peace I give to you.*[Jn.14:27] He said: *I have spoken to you, that in me you might have peace.*[Jn.16:33]

Real peace only comes with Christ's pardon and salvation. In sin you can never have peace in your spirit. The Bible says: *There is no peace, says my God, to the wicked.*[Is.57:21] But *being justified by faith, we have peace with God through our Lord Jesus Christ.*[Ro.5:1]

Are you longing for His peace in you?

FOURTH: It means to have fellowship with God.

You were created in God's likeness,[Ge.1:27] so you could walk and talk with God.[1Jn.1:3] But sin separated you from God.[Is.59:2] Now, instead of fellowship with the Father, you fear God; the thought of facing Him frightens you.[Ro.14:10-12; 2Pe.3:7-8; Jude 14-15] Sin condemns you and causes you to be guilty before God.[Jn.3:18; Ro.5:12,18]

Only Christ can save you from your sins.[Mt.1:21; Ac.4:12] He will blot out every stain and bring you back to God with a clear record — as if you had never sinned. Then you can say with John: *Truly our fellowship is with the Father, and with his Son Jesus Christ.*[1Jn.1:3] He will be *a friend that sticks closer than a brother or a sister.*[Pr.18:24] You can receive Him today.

FIFTH: To be saved means to receive physical healing.

The Bible says: *You shall serve the Lord your God, and I will take sickness away from the midst of you.*[Ex.23:25]

The Bible says: *Who forgives all your iniquities; who heals all your diseases.*[Ps.103:3]

Salvation includes physical healing and mental soundness. To be saved means to be made whole spiritually and physically.

In the gospels, Christ always forgave sinners and healed the sick, and He *is the same yesterday, and today, and forever.*[He.13:8]

Christ has come to save you today. *Behold, now is the accepted time; behold, now is the day of salvation.*[2Co.6:2]

You can receive Him now. You can become a real Christian. You can be saved.

What is a real Christian?

According to the Bible, a real Christian is a person who (1) has come to God unconverted; (2) accepted by faith the Lord Jesus Christ as personal

Savior, by surrendering to Him as Lord and master; (3) confesses Christ as Lord before the world, and then (4) strives to please Him in everything, every day of their life.

If you are not sure that you have personally accepted Jesus Christ into your heart as your Lord and master, then I joyfully point to you the way to peace with God, forgiveness of sins, and to the great joy of living the Christ-life.

FIRST: Realize that you have sinned. *All have sinned and come short of the glory of God.*[Ro.3:23] *If we say that we have no sin, we deceive ourselves.*[1Jn.1:8]

SECOND: Truly be sorry for and repent of your sins. *And the publican, standing afar off, would not lift up so much as his eyes to heaven, but smote his breast, saying, God be merciful to me a sinner.*[Lu.18:13] *For godly sorrow works repentance to salvation.*[2Co.7:10]

THIRD: Confess your sins to God. *If you cover your sins, you shall not prosper: but if you confess and forsake them, you shall have mercy.*[Pr.28:13] *If we confess our sins* (to Him), *he is faithful and just to forgive us our sins, and to cleanse us from all unrighteousness.*[1Jn.1:9]

FOURTH: Forsake your sins or put them away. *Let the wicked forsake their ways, and the unrighteous their thoughts: and let them return to the Lord, and he will have mercy on them, for he will abundantly pardon.*[Is.55:7] *If you confess and forsake your sins, you shall have mercy.*[Pr.28:13]

FIFTH: Ask forgiveness for your sins. *Who forgives all your iniquities.*[Ps.103:3] *Come now and let us reason together, says the Lord: Though your sins be as scarlet, they shall be as white as snow; though they be red like crimson, they shall be as wool.*[Is.1:18]

SIXTH: Consecrate your entire life to Christ. *Whoever, therefore, shall confess me before others, I will confess that one before my Father which is in heaven.*[Mt.10:32] *But you are a chosen generation that you should show forth the praises of him who has called you out of darkness to his marvelous light.*[1Pe.2:9]

SEVENTH: *Believe that God saves you by His grace. For by grace are you saved through faith; and that not of yourselves: it is the gift of God: Not of works, lest any one should boast.*[Ep.2:8-9; 1Jn.2:12; Ep.1:7]

Right now, find a place alone with God, get on your knees and pray to the Lord this prayer right out loud.

O Lord in heaven:

I do, here and now, believe on Jesus Christ, the Son of God. I believe that in Your great mercy and love, You died for me, as my personal substitute.

I believe that You suffered all of the penalty of my sins and that You paid the full price so that there is no more sin laid to my charge.

What love You manifested toward me, O Lord.

You were perfectly innocent. I was the guilty

one. I had broken God's law. I should have been crucified. But You loved me too much to let me die for my own sins. How I thank You for taking my place and for paying my full debt.

When You suffered my penalty, I was freed. There remain no sins to condemn me, so there is now no reason for me to be guilty before God. I can never be judged or sentenced for the sins which You died for. They were judged in You, Lord.

All of my sins and old nature were put on Your account and You paid it all for me. Now all of Your spotless righteousness is put to my account, so that I am now redeemed and saved.

Lord, I believe on Jesus Christ.

I do, here and now, welcome You into my heart as my Savior from sin, from hell, and from all the power of the devil.

I accept You, Jesus, as Lord of my life, and here and now devote myself to pleasing You. Jesus Christ, You have said that if I would come to You, You would not cast me out. I have come to You with all my heart, as a helpless, guilty sinner, seeking salvation, and trusting only in Your blood.

I trust that the blood of Jesus Christ blots out every sin and transgression from my life.

I trust that You did enough for me; that You

paid the full price for my transgressions, and that there can never be any further price for me to pay. You paid it all.

I trust in Your redemption of my soul.

I trust that I am saved, by calling on the name of the Lord.

I shall never make another effort or claim any merit, or pay any price, or offer any good works, nor shall I ever — as long as I live — think or say or do anything more to have my past sins forgiven, or to be saved.

Dear Lord, You did enough, nearly 2,000 years ago. You paid the full price for all of my sins, and for my salvation forever.

So from this day, I trust in what You did for me at the cross. It is enough. I am saved because of what You did for me. Nothing can ever improve my salvation.

You were wounded for my transgressions; You were bruised for my iniquities. The punishment I ought to have endured was laid upon You and You bore it for me.

I am now saved.

From this moment, I shall strive to follow You and to share the good news with others so that they can receive Your life too.

Thank You, Lord, for my full salvation.

I am redeemed. My sins are forgiven. They can never condemn me again. I am saved. I believe on Jesus Christ. I trust in all You have done for me. It is enough. I am at peace. I am free from guilt and condemnation. I am a Christian – a follower of Jesus Christ, the Son of God.

Praise the Lord. Jesus saves me now.

Amen.

Now your sins are forgiven.[Co.1:14] Your name is written in God's book of life.[Re.21:27] Only believe. Jesus lives in you now.[Ga.2:20] You have His life.[1Jn.5:12]

Begin your new life by reading the gospels of Jesus and by praying every day. Tell others about your new life and become a partner in reaching others for Christ.

A new miracle life has begun for you. I would be very pleased if you would write me a personal letter and tell me that you have been saved.

From the time we hear from you, my wife and I will be on our knees every morning, praying and believing for God's very best for you and your house.

As an act of faith, register your decision below. Be definite about it. Receiving Christ as your Savior is the greatest miracle of your life.

If you believe the Bible promises contained in

this book and if you have sincerely prayed and received Jesus into your life by faith, then an angel is recording your name *in the Lamb's book of life,*[Re.21:27] right now.

Registering your decision below will be a lasting testimony of your personal experience today. If your enemy, the devil, ever tries to make you doubt what has taken place, you will refer to the decision you recorded this day, and know that you have received the abundant life of Jesus Christ and have been born again.

MY DECISION

Today I have read this book, *The Good Life.* I have learned what it means to be saved. I have sincerely taken the steps outlined in this book and I have reverently prayed the prayer that is written here.

I believe I have received Jesus Christ in my own life and that I am reborn with His life. I commit my life to do my best to please Him in all that I think and say and do. With His grace and help, I shall share Jesus Christ with others.

Relying on Him to keep me by His grace, I have made this decision today — in Jesus' name.

Signed ________________________________

Date __________________________

Now seal your decision and confession, by writing me a personal letter to tell me that you have accepted Jesus Christ, and that you have received the miracle of the new birth.

My wife and I pray for every person who reads this book. Our greatest reward is to receive letters from those who have been reborn as a result.

We will answer you personally, and we shall then become prayer partners in following and serving Jesus Christ.

We are praying for you.

T. L. Osborn

NOTES

NOTES

NOTES

NOTES

GLOBAL PUBLISHER

OSBORN PUBLICATIONS
P.O. Box 10
Tulsa, OK 74102 USA

✧✧✧

FRENCH DISTRIBUTOR

ÉDITIONS
MINISTÈRES MULTILINGUES
909, Boul. Roland-Therrien
Longueuil, Québec J4J 4L3 Canada

✧✧✧

GERMAN PUBLISHER

SHALOM — VERLAG
Pachlinger Strrasse 10
D-93486 Runding, CHAM, Germany

✧✧✧

PORTUGUESE PUBLISHER

GRACA EDITORIAL
Caixa Postal 1815
Rio de Janiero–RJ–20001, Brazil

✧✧✧

SPANISH PUBLISHER

LIBROS DESAFIO, Apdo. 29724
Bogota, Colombia

(For Quantity Orders, Request Discount Prices.)